Out-of-Body Experiences
A *Handbook*

by

Janet Lee Mitchell

McFarland & Company, Inc.
Jefferson, N.C., & London
1981

Library of Congress Cataloging in Publication Data

Mitchell, Janet Lee
   Out-of-body experiences.

      Bibliography: p.
      Includes index.
      1. Astral projection. I. Title.
   BF1389.A7M55   133.9   81-8145   AACR2

ISBN 0-89950-031-5

Manufactured in the United States of America

To Aline

Table of Contents

Acknowledgments

If it were not for Ingo Swann, this book would not have been written. He came to the American Society for Psychical Research in 1971 when my dedication to parapsychological ideas was eroding. He showed me that these types of experiences are real and can be valuable. He told me I could write a book and I believed him. I am grateful to him for his inspiration and for sharing some of his fascinating inner life with me.

Joan Ann de Mattia has been a steady support for my work since 1974. She has provided me with food and shelter in times of dire need. She has always been a true friend and a wonderful sister.

Special thanks for encouragement and professional advice to Ruth Hagy Brod, Lee C. Downing, Eleanor Friede, Marian Nester, Karlis Osis, Boneita Perskari, Gertrude Schmeidler, and Elsie West.

Foreword

by Gertrude Schmeidler

This is a book about an extraordinary, even a shocking possibility. It suggests that a person's conscious awareness can detach itself from the person's body, can travel to another place, can observe what is happening there, and sometimes can even produce a physical change at that distant place.

Is this believable? Is it science, or only science fantasy? You will reach your own decision as you read about it (or perhaps like me will arrive only at a state of indecision). You will of course examine the material critically to decide between accepting or discounting the evidence for this bizarre claim. Let me introduce it by suggesting an analogy.

Suppose someone, face to face, tells you a story so utterly unlike anything in your own experience that it sounds like a dream or a fairy tale. Will you reject the story as untrue?

You might. Probably you would if the person speaking to you was a stranger who came to you without credentials. You might suspect he was planning a fraud to victimize you, or that he was a prankster enjoying a joke at your expense, or that he was deluded, perhaps insane. It's easy to dismiss a stranger's story, and it may be similarly easy for you to dismiss some of what follows in this book.

But suppose that the person is someone you know and trust or who is trusted by others whose opinions you respect. And suppose that by every other sign you could ask for, the person seems sensible, honest, intelligent, self-critical. This seems to me to apply to some of the people whose accounts are reported in this book: men of fine professional reputation, whose other work and whose personal lives would, in my opinion, make us think we could depend on the accuracy of what they say. If you would ordinarily accept without question what a person tells you, will you be willing to stretch the bounds of your belief for his unlikely tale?

Well, yes, any of us might stretch those bounds a little. If someone we know to be reliable told us that a stranger walked up to him on the street, gave him a thousand dollars and walked away, we might continue to think that our informant was sane and accurate and that the improbable incident really happened.

Suppose however that the reliable informant told us something not merely improbable but something we thought was impossible? Would we change our opinion of what was possible or change our opinion of the informant? What if others we respect support his story and tell similar stories of their own? How much and what kind of evidence can persuade us to rethink something we have always taken for granted?

Here is a book that will test your reactions. A typical story in it is that a person while in bed one night found himself looking from another vantage point at his own body, then found himself in another place. He was not dreaming. He could see what was happening around him. After a time he found he was back in his own room, saw his own body, and went back into it. Further, some of the stories tell us that what the person had seen in that distant place was actually there.

Can you believe this? I couldn't, some years ago; but I'm now in the uncomfortable position of not knowing whether I can or not. Common sense says it's absurd, and common sense is usually right — but there are times when it's wrong.

Let's consider the claims in terms of the general issue of what might compel us to accept something that seems incredible. One reason might be the evidence of our own senses. We've probably all laughed at the old joke of the rustic who disbelieved what his eyes told him, when he went to his first carnival. He looked for a long time at the giraffe who was moving around, and finally said, "There ain't no such animal." If any of us had traveled to a distant place while our body stayed in bed, it would be easy to believe that others had done so. But I haven't. For me, the evidence of my own experience doesn't support the claim.

Surely a second reason that could make us believe what common sense denies is scientific evidence. Our senses tell us a table is solid; molecular theory and atomic theory, with the weight of all authorities in physics behind them, have convinced us that the table is composed of tiny molecules with wide spaces between them, rather than a continuous surface, and also that what we used to call solid particles are better described as electromagnetic fields. Against the evidence of our senses, we believe that the earth revolves around the sun, or that the sun and earth revolve around a common center of gravity, not that the earth stands still while heavenly bodies move. But does the scientific establishment tell us that a man can leave his body, or a woman can leave hers, go to a distant place, then return to the body? No; far from it. Science-with-a-capital-S, as shown in standard textbooks, either disregards such claims or treats them with disdain.

What else might persuade us to believe? Our religion, or perhaps the authority of those we trust. But these are personal matters that vary from one individual to the next.

I will suggest one last possible reason for accepting something as true. It stems from two sources: our recognition that science moves slowly, and our recognition that scientific evidence has established much that earlier wisdom used to dismiss as false. Probably we all accept in principle the idea that future discoveries will teach us new truths, not yet established. Could it be that the claim of out-of-body travel is one of these truths which is now only in the early stages of being investigated? If we ourselves look at the evidence, will it seem so strong that we are sure it will later be generally considered valid?

This is Dr. Mitchell's opinion. She first regarded the claims with disbelief, but as she learned more of the facts she felt obliged to change her mind. She spreads the material before us in this book, and tries to present the whole case dispassionately, showing both the arguments for discrediting the claims and the facts and arguments that speak for them. She does it well, I think, especially as she always makes clear to the reader where her own opinion lies.

As for me, I do not know. Let me put the case before you in brief, even though the book does it better, at length.

Many people of excellent reputation and critical intelligence have not only reported out-of-body experiences but have also tested them sufficiently to become convinced that they have actually traveled away from where their bodies were. Some few carefully controlled laboratory experiments have collected data consistent with this claim. I do not doubt the honesty of the laboratory workers or of many of the experiencers; I am willing to accept as fact a very substantial number of the accounts.

ix

But having accepted the facts, can I explain them in some other way? Can I still hold firm to my old assumption that the living consciousness stays where the body is? Yes, but not easily. I must strain for it.

How do I account for the out-of-body experiencer reporting accurately some fact that occurred elsewhere? If the fact is not too unusual, I call it simple coincidence, inference, guesswork. And when the fact is so unusual that it cannot be dismissed this way, I call it ESP — ESP with a fantasy surrounding it. My analogy is to the cases that have been reported where a sleeping person is awakened by having water sprinkled on him. A few seconds after the drops fall on him, he wakes up, but in those few seconds he may have dreamed of taking his morning shower, or being caught in a rainstorm. The sensory information about water droplets has been cloaked in a fantasy. It seems straightforward to argue that ESP information about a distant place may be similarly cloaked in the fantasy of having traveled there.

How do I account for the out-of-body experiencer having been seen at the distant place, by another person? That's considerably harder, but I can stretch the ESP explanation to think that perhaps the out-of-body experiencer had such a strong telepathic influence upon the other person as to make that person have a dreamlike fantasy which corresponded to his or her own. It seems unlikely, but surely it is no more unlikely than true out-of-body travel.

And how account for the recently reported findings that an instrument recorded physical changes in a place at the same time that the out-of-body experiencer saw what was at that place? Perhaps I could argue that the experiencer was simultaneously using both psychokinesis to influence the instrument and ESP to obtain the information, even though such conjunction of psychokinesis and ESP has never been shown to occur.

By stretching and straining, by introducing a new interpretation to accommodate each new bit of evidence, I can explain each bit away. But the process is uncomfortably reminiscent of the way conservative scientists used to produce a new theory to explain away each new meteorite that was found, rather than believing the impossible explanation that stones fall from the sky.

So there I stay, awkwardly balanced on the fence. On one

side of the fence is acceptance of a radical new concept of human potential, and on the other side is a series of disconnected, rather implausible interpretations. I do not know which way to go. When you read Dr. Mitchell's book you will be able to judge for yourself whether this reluctance to accept the out-of-body interpretation is wise or foolish. More important, you will judge whether our common sense ideas of the relationship between mind and body do or do not need some radical rethinking.

*Where there is no vision,
the people perish.* (Proverbs 29:18)

Chapter I

He Can See What
Others Say He Cannot

If I had never met Ingo Swann, I would not have written
this book, much less begun to think seriously about out-of-body
experiences (OBES). I was unaware of such types of experiences
and when I first heard of them in 1967, I certainly didn't believe
such a thing was possible in my wildest imagination. I have never
had an OBE that could be validated objectively, but I have come
to believe that it is possible for someone's consciousness actually
to perceive from a point of view outside of visual range. And if
this is indeed a fact, it may constitute the most important experience for us to understand, whether we are parapsychologists
engaged in a scientific study or any other human being who
wonders if we are or are not limited to purely physical or sense
perceptions.

Ingo Swann is, by far, the most talented psi performer I
have ever had the opportunity to work with and observe.
Whereas some may consider the psi results he obtained at the
American Society for Psychical Research a myth, I was there and
it was as real as breathing. This is not to discredit the value of
myths for the beginning of our understanding of psychic
behavior. Most scientific discoveries evolve from myths. Examples might be archaeologists' discovery of Troy, or discoveries
that the earth is round or that it revolves around the sun.

Swann was born in Telluride, Colorado, on September
14, 1933. He is of Swedish descent. He stresses the idea that one's
basic nature is spiritual and that humanity "is obliged to move
forward into the study and application of greater areas of human
and spiritual potential."

1

He has said that his first out-of-body experience happened at the age of three. During a tonsillectomy, while under anesthesia, he says he watched the doctor perform the operation and was able afterward to report accurately to the doctor some of the smallest details of the operation. After this event, his OBES seem to have occurred spontaneously. When he was eight years old, he witnessed a childhood friend being killed in a high fall. This traumatic event brought about for the first time an awareness of the destructibility of the physical body, and seemed to suppress his ability to perceive outside of visual range for many years.

As a young soldier in Korea in 1957, he was pondering what direction his life should take. He is a pensive man of high intelligence who can pick up the terminology of a given subject almost immediately, which facilitates his gaining knowledge in an area rapidly. As he sat on a hilltop in Korea, he had a spiritual experience that he says, "brought about an intense uplifting of awareness and a seemingly mature out-of-body experience."

After returning home, he wrote, painted, and took a job at the United Nations. In 1968 he resigned a position at the United Nations Secretariat he had held for over ten years, and turned his attention to rehabilitating his psychic and creative abilities.

I first met Ingo Swann in the fall of 1971. He had been experimenting on his own for several years with what he called "exterior vision." He had been practicing this type of vision intensely since July 1971. There were multiple areas of confusion for him at this time. Sometimes his vision would be white; sometimes black. He told me once that for nine days he kept getting back into his body upside down. In this condition, his vision would be upside down, then everything would collapse, turn black, and then return to normal vision.

When he was sharpening his ability to see at a distance, he would decide to place his vision, or a part of his consciousness, at some public place and note down details he perceived there. When he traveled in this way, there was no apparent means of navigation. He simply decided to go some place and suddenly found himself there. Later he would actually go to these places to see if his notes were correct. For example, he would identify materials in store window displays or examine architectural details of unfamiliar buildings.

Swann has said the stages in his development went something like this:

(1) "Hey, how about that, I can do it!" Stimulated and happy. If done at night, inability to sleep from the excitement.

(2) "Well, I did it again." Impressed but not too excited anymore.

(3) "Why the hell can't I do it every time?" Aggravated and frustrated. If done at night, inability to sleep because of failure.

I asked him what he felt about his body when he was elsewhere. He replied that it was like a precious piece of furniture to which he was very attached. He could sometimes smell or hear while out of his body but the senses of taste and touch had not been operative at the time of our experiments. He definitely felt that he had the ability to speak through his body while being exterior to it.

He practiced for about three years on his own before he felt the ability was consistent enough to operate successfully under laboratory conditions. He was also curious as to how his brain waves looked when he was doing this successfully. The American Society for Psychical Research (ASPR) had just begun a talent search for those who felt they had had an OBE and could reproduce one in the lab. I was interested in physiological activity during OBEs and I could provide him with information on his brain waves if he could give me information on targets outside of visual range. It was a mutually beneficial relationship and I enjoyed working with him.

Our first attempts at the ASPR to develop methodology by which we could ascertain whether a person could localize part of his or her consciousness in space some distance from the body were perceptual organization tests. We placed two two-inch deep target boxes on a platform which was ten feet above the floor of the experimental room where Swann sat. There was a partition between the two boxes so if his point of view was from one end of the platform, he could only see the target on that side if his exterior vision operated like normal vision. These targets could have been perceived telepathically, clairvoyantly, precognitively, or fraudulently, but I have reasons to believe that they were perceived by some type of perception which operated outside of normal visual range.

I was convinced of his ability after about six months of

working closely with him two or three days a week. Here are some of the reasons I thought this type of vision was closer to normal vision than to extrasensory perception (ESP).

(1) Lighting arrangements had to be adjusted to accommodate the exterior vision. Certain glaring lights, such as spotlights, reportedly cast shadows or light rays over target material which could not be seen through. Soft, diffuse lights were ultimately chosen to be placed about two feet above target material and then vision became easier.

(2) Some colors were more easily recognized than others. For example, black, red, white, blue, and green could usually be distinguished but pastels and colors such as orange, pink, and lavender were difficult to distinguish. Targets were therefore usually in primary colors to aid the vision.

(3) Three-dimensional targets were not easier to see. Flat cutouts or drawings were preferred.

(4) Whole figures seemed to work better than outlines.

(5) Target materials that absorbed light worked better than reflective materials. Construction paper in primary colors was therefore chosen as the optimum target material. Other materials that were identified were leather, fabrics, and clay. Materials that were difficult included metal, plastic, glossy photographs, and a glass of water.

(6) Simple shapes and strong familiar forms were easier to perceive than strange conglomerations or unfamiliar forms of groupings.

(7) Letters and numbers were seen only as shapes and often not seen.

(8) There were days when his exterior vision was cloudy, which he called "black and white" days. He had a certainty about his vision that is seldom seen in ESP confidence calls. He filled out questionnaires as to how good or bad his exterior vision was on a specific day (before seeing the targets, of course) and these questionnaires were correlated with his actual score on a given day—that is, whether he reproduced the target or not in his response. The data indicate that he knew when he could see and when he could not but it is still a mystery why the visual capacity fluctuates. There were hints that high humidity had an adverse effect, so in future experiments barometrical readings should be included in data. Moods and other psychological variables such as motivation and novelty of experiment seemed to

affect results. Swann said he felt his vision was impaired by a poor sense of security, hostile surroundings (demanding proof of his ability), and physical illness of any kind.

A typical experiment of this early exploratory type would go something like this: Swann would arrive at the lab and I would place electrodes on his body to record and measure bodily functions when he reported being out of his body. Regular recordings were taken of the left and right occipital lobes of his brain (the back of the cortex where vision is organized). Other physiological measurements such as heart rate, blood volume, muscle tension, and eye movements varied on different days.

We would then enter a locked room where targets had been placed on the previously described platform suspended from the ceiling. I never knew what the targets were beforehand and it was often extremely exciting for both of us to see the similarities between target and response after the experiment. I would plug the leads from the electrodes on his scalp into a junction box which led to a polygraph machine in the adjoining room. His movements were therefore controlled all the time he was in the room, since any movement from the chair would disconnect the equipment.

I then left him alone and went in the adjoining room to monitor the polygraph. He could take as much time as he needed to "view" the targets, make comments over an intercom system that would be recorded on the EEG record, and make a drawing of what he saw. When he felt he had seen as much as he could, he would tell me over the intercom and I would go in and disconnect him from the equipment. I would then get a ladder from another floor of the building, climb up, and bring the targets down for comparison with his response.

This was the best method for obtaining positive results and one judge, who was unaware of the type of experiment she was judging, correctly matched eight sets of targets and responses. The expectation of this happening by chance is about 1 in 40,000. But novelty is important in these types of experiments so that boredom will not set in and cause scores to decline. Also, since this was an exploratory time, we tried many other techniques. One-shot trials do not lead to statistical analysis, but it seemed more important to keep our enthusiasm high in our quest to determine what would work best.

Dr. Carole (Silfen) Kendig, perceptual psychologist from

Seton Hall University, brought in some of the most interesting equipment. Regular perceptual tests were administered, but with the testing devices outside of visual range. One test involved brightness comparison between two luminous displays and after analyzing three preliminary sessions, Kendig felt Swann's judgment curves would gradually approximate the curve produced with normal vision. His sensitivity would fluctuate from session to session. Results suggested that perceptual learning might take place under these conditions. In most perceptual learning experiments, several hundred trials are often conducted before there is a significant shift in accuracy of judgment and we were unable to obtain the number of trials necessary to make our findings conclusive.

Using another multipurpose perceptual device, which presented two transparent static figures of a galloping horse flashing alternately in different locations, Ingo could report whether the figures were blinking on and off or not. The device was not only outside his visual range, but he preferred to be blindfolded during these sessions to help keep his eyes from moving. Since perception of *phi* movement (lights blinking on and off so as to appear to be moving, as on a theatre marquee) and critical flicker/fusion did occur, there is the suggestion that Swann's exterior perception may be organized in a fashion similar to that of normal visual perception.

Kendig also made a covered viewing box with windows on two walls. When you looked through one window, you saw one display and when you looked through the other window, you saw something different. Other devices that were tried included boxes with a mirrored wall reflecting a target which could be seen through an aperture in the box. One device displayed geometrical slides through a small opening. Swann expressed the opinion that a smaller opening somehow concentrated his "attention units" used for viewing and he felt he could see better in this situation than when he was asked to perceive something in a room where he would have to begin with a wide angle view and then zero in and try to condense his point of view, which would be disbursed in the room.

There was a definite learning process involved in Swann's identifying the platform targets. These experiments were continued over six months' time. Other experimental efforts may have been tried for one or two days and the results cannot be expected to be as good when there is no time for getting accustomed to the new task or learning to adjust the vision under the various circumstances.

Many days were spent helping him learn how to improve his vision. For instance, he might just want to try to see lighted targets on a five-color machine called an ESPatester. He had trouble with color discriminations between white and yellow, and blue and green. One time he was able to discriminate purple stripes on a black background, which we both felt was remarkable. When he was not concerned about color perception, he sometimes only requested brain-wave feedback in different frequency bands of activity to ascertain how his exterior vision might be improved in this way. We always tried to cooperate to give him any help he felt he needed.

Sometimes Dr. Karlis Osis, Director of Research at the ASPR, would decide to send an assistant to a local museum and have Swann try to find her there and tell what she was looking at. Swann sometimes liked to look around in Arizona and once gave us a weather report on Tucson. The more variety, the better he liked it.[1]

I feel that one can and probably should change experimental conditions as one continues but not quite so radically as we did. Visual tasks could be changed gradually from simple to more complex target material. For instance, as one is able to correctly identify color, shape could be introduced.

When we first started the experiments on "astral projection," I was skeptical and not at all sure that such a thing occurred. My main interest therefore was recording physiological measurements while people reported being out of body to see if any physical patterns would emerge during these times.

Ingo was given an electronic button to push to register on the EEG when he felt he had been exterior to his body. In another series of experiments, I would designate alternate one-minute intervals in which he should try to exteriorize or rest. The EEGs were recorded in 39 sessions from November 1971 through May 1972.

In order to analyze the records, one-minute periods of reported OBE and control periods were marked off on the EEG. An assistant and myself scored these records without knowledge of which periods were which. Forty-five periods of OBE were compared to 36 control periods.

The EEG records of both the right and left hemispheres of

Ingo's brain were studied. Overall statistics revealed that during the out-of-body condition, whether he reported it or I directed it, there was some sort of loss of electrical activity. Overall frequency data showed a *decrease* in alpha activity during the out-of-body state. This decrease was more marked in the right than the left hemisphere. The statistical probability that the mean amplitude decreases would occur by chance was calculated at 1000 to 1 on the right side and 200 to 1 on the left side.

Therefore, when he said he was out of his body, or even when I signalled him to exteriorize, there was a loss of electrical activity and a speed-up of the brain waves in the visual, occipital region of his brain. His heart rate and other functions of the autonomic nervous system remained normal.

From electroculograph (EOG) records, it appeared there was usually a cessation of eye movements when Swann reported being out. He felt that eye movements distracted the OBE vision in some way. Both Tart[2] and Morris et al.[3] found substantial decreases in rapid eye movements (REM) during OBE. This seems to indicate that the OBE state is different from dreaming or daydreaming where an increase of REM is characteristic.

Amplitude (voltage) decreases in EEGs have been reported in connection with experiences that might be related in some way to OBES. For instance, Spencer Sherman did a study of experiential and electroencephalographic patterns and characteristics of people in very deep hypnosis.[4] Characteristic experiences of very deep hypnosis showed many correlations to out-of-body reports, such as "feeling totally free, complete loss of touch with external environment, feeling of motion, feeling totally spread out, mind fully separated and physically distant from body." Not only were the experiences similar, but the EEG data reflected essentially the same findings as reported above. At very deep points (of hypnosis), the amplitude of the EEG, from both vertex and occipital electrode loci, showed periods of drastic decrease.

Dr. Elmer Green and associates at the Menninger Foundation worked with Swami Rama, who demonstrated an outstanding ability to control his own physiology.[5] During Swami Rama's "control of heart" tests, his EEG showed a large decrease of amplitude as compared to a resting period.

Voltage indications provided by electrodes on the outside of the scalp can reflect only the average electrical state of millions of neurons over a large portion of the brain. Interpretation of a voltage decrease in an EEG is therefore extremely difficult. I believe it is worthwhile to pursue this approach in order to check on the accuracy of this finding. Morris et al.[3] reported EEG alpha decreases and Tart[2] reported a flattening of the EEG, both of which are indicative of voltage decreases. Because of the differences in individual EEGs, type of equipment used, electrode placement, methods of evaluation, and experimenter effects, another pattern may emerge in the study of another individual. Replication of such studies are very much needed, however.

An intriguing experimental idea may be to have the experient (one who has the experience of being out of body) in a room where electromagnetic measurements can be taken of the entire space or any segment thereof. The question to be answered would be, if one's EEG indicated a loss of electrical energy in the brain, could a voltage increase be measured near the body or in the room? We may be able to actually track the energy in this way or localize the out-of-body entity.

In the summer of 1972 Swann did a series of experiments at Stanford Research Institute. He returned to the ASPR in the fall and we began work with a new optical image device (OID) designed and built by Len Barkus and James Merewether. Osis describes the OID as "an apparatus for the display of stimulus pictures which appear in a viewing window in random order. The target pictures consist of three aspects: color of the background (green, blue, red, or black), quadrant of the background (upper left, lower left, lower right, or upper right), and line drawings of five different images. The final composite picture is not located in its complete form in any part of the apparatus, but appears as an optical illusion, visible only from a location directly in front of the viewing window."

Ingo Swann familiarized himself with the OID for several days in order to get used to the new lighting conditions and the way the target material was presented. The OID was located in an adjoining room with the door closed. At first when Swann tried to ascertain the different aspects of the target outside of visual range, he experienced many reversals of position. For instance, he would think it was in the lower left when in fact it would be in the upper right quadrant. Arrows were placed on the front of the device to help him get oriented in front of the target. Later a little light was placed inside on the floor of the box. Sometimes Swann would feel nauseated or get fatigued from trying to perceive targets on the round background divided into different-colored quadrants with the bright light projecting an image on first one and then another of the quadrants. Maintaining a stable point of view was all important in these tests and fatigue seemed to break down his ability to stabilize his vision.

After doing tests with feedback on the device for a little over a week, Swann started to get statistically significant results in some sessions. Again, his vision fluctuated from day to day. By analyzing a block of 144 trials after he felt he could perceive the new target, results showed that he got enough three-aspect hits (color, symbol, and quadrant) that odds against a chance for such results were 1 in 100.

I think these results and his cooperation were outstanding considering the inherent difficulties in pioneering efforts. Time must be allowed for necessary alterations and adjustments so that conditions will be tolerable, if not comfortable, and productive for all those involved.

End Notes

[1]For Swann's version of his work at the ASPR, see his auto-biography *To Kiss Earth Good-Bye* (New York: Hawthorn Books, 1975).

[2]Charles Tart, "A Psychophysiological Study of Out-of-the-Body Experiences in a Selected Subject," *Journal of the American Society for Psychical Research* **62** (1968):3-27.

[3]A more detailed, scientific write-up of the Harary experiments can be found in R.L. Morris et al., "Studies of Communication during Out-of-Body Experiences," *Journal of the American Society for Psychical Research* **72** (1978):1-21.

[4]Spencer Sherman, "Brief Report: Very Deep Hypnosis," *Journal of Transpersonal Psychology* **1** (1972):87-91. This is a synopsis of his dissertation dealing with subjects who experience feelings character-istic of OBEs during deep hypnosis.

[5]E.E. Green et al., "Voluntary Controls Project: Swami Rama. Preliminary Report," Menninger Foundation, 6 June 1970.

Chapter II
What Brings It On?

Some people consciously desire an OBE and use various methods and techniques to bring it about. They are usually pleased to have achieved their goal and to have satisfied a point of curiosity. Others feel as if they were catapulted from their bodies at a time of grave danger from accidents, operations, or serious illnesses. These people usually experience some relief, or at least pain and fear, as a result of this reaction to danger. But most people who have an OBE have a spontaneous experience and have never heard of such a thing occurring. What happens to them?

There are several possibilities. It may have such an impact on their thought processes that, whereas they may never discuss it with anyone nor be able to, their whole view of life and death may be altered from that day forward. Most, however, probably just forget about it entirely, call it a dream, or invalidate it with any number of rationalizations. If it cannot be repressed or suppressed by an individual in any of these ways, the person's physical health may be put into question. For instance, one may think it was just a result of too high or too low blood pressure. If physical examinations are all negative, and spontaneous experiences continue and no one understands what you are talking about (if you have nerve enough to discuss it), your next logical assumption would probably be that you are losing your grip. An uninformed therapist might agree with you on consultation and you may end up on a locked neuropsychiatric ward with other people "controlling" your body. Tragedies like this undoubtedly occur. It is well to remember that if *anyone* can control your body *you* can.

That is why it is so important that people know that these

experiences of being separate from one's body have been reported for hundreds, even thousands of years by all strata of society, including the sane and "normal." If this book reaches the hands of one individual who is confused and distressed by an OBE that can neither be named nor understood, then it has served its purpose. Therefore, remembering that most OBES are spontaneous and without known cause, we shall examine some of the conditions and states of consciousness which seem conducive to OBES.

Sleep and Dreams

As you will see in Chapter VI, the dream state could be an unconscious OBE. It is not unusual then that we find many unconscious OBES evolving from sleep and dream states. For instance, have you ever had a dream of falling or flying? It has been suggested that these dreams of moving freely through space could be unconscious OBES themselves, memories of unconscious OBES, or test runs for future conscious OBES. Flying dreams are usually exhilarating and give one a sense of power. Falling dreams bring about the opposite emotions of fear and insecurity. Fear of not being able to get back into the body during an OBE seems to be the major block to consciously realizing a personal OBE.

Hypothetically, a dream sequence with an OBE emerging could go something like this: I become aware of flying while asleep. It feels great and I am having a wonderful time. It really feels as if I can do this. Maybe I should go show someone. As consciousness begins to emerge, fear strikes, "Oh my God, where is my body?" With this thought the out-of-body entity returns instantaneously and I may even experience "falling to my death," however I never hit the ground, but wake up safe and sound in my own body in my own bed.

This is only a hypothetical dream situation. Usually one only remembers the flying segment or the falling segment. The part of the experience that you become conscious of in the dream may be influenced by your moods and attitudes on retiring. If you are enduring more stress than usual, the fear elements may be remembered, but not the free, exhilarated feelings.

There is another type of dream that figures in OBES. Have you ever dreamed, become conscious that you were dreaming, and taken some control over the dream? A dream that you become conscious of and exert some control over is called a lucid dream. Some students of OBEs believe the lucid dream is the best launching pad for a fully conscious OBE. It seems similarly effective to become conscious of and gain control over the imagery one experiences just before going to sleep or awakening.

Fatigue

Exhaustion can be enough to break down the emotional barriers causing a person to cling to the idea that they live, move, and have their being within a body. How many of you have come in exhausted, flopped down on a couch or bed and passed out immediately, only to find that shortly thereafter you physically jerked back to conscious awareness? Sylvan Muldoon had some interesting comments on what I assumed to be muscle spasms:

> There are hundreds of people, yes, everyone who sleeps, whose astral bodies move slightly out of coincidence for the purpose of becoming charged with cosmic energy every night. Have you ever noticed that, when greatly fatigued and in the hypnagogic state, just entering sleep, you have suddenly given a spasmodic jumping and become conscious? The doctor calls it "nerves," but that explains nothing. The solution of the problem is simple. When the condenser of cosmic energy, the astral body, is run down, the subconscious moves it out of coincidence as soon as possible to enable it to recuperate more quickly. So, when fatigued ... the astral body moves out of coincidence.... A sudden noise or an emotion, such as fear, and the astral body repercusses, shocking the physical body — although it may not have been separated more than a few inches from it.[1]

There are cases where people have thought they awoke from deep sleep and got up, only to find their bodies still asleep on the bed and themselves rather confused as to this state of affairs. Sometimes fretful sleep is a result of extreme fatigue and a nightmare may become so intolerable that the sleeper projects in order to escape supposed imminent danger.

Drugs

Out-of-body experiences are frequently reported under general anesthesia, especially in a stressful situation such as in the dentist's chair. Nitrous oxide (gas) can bring about many changes in the perception of one's own body, including being some distance from it with the ability to observe it as another person.

Psychedelic drugs sometimes produce effects similar to OBES. This is not always the case, as one study by McGlothlin and Gatozzi shows. They obtained data from 247 LSD users. They found that hallucinogenic drugs could induce feelings of being separate from the body but it happened only about 3 to 4 percent of the time. It was not a constant, predicted effect of these drugs.

Shamans and other members of non-Western cultures use a variety of hallucinogenic herbs to induce OBE states. It is a widespread, accepted religious ritual. Almost every known human society has used some mood-altering substance to escape from the workaday world.

Drugs such as LSD, mescaline, and psilocybin have a tendency to increase one's temperature and it may be this aspect of the drug that induces the OBE, because a high fever can also bring about an OBE.

Sensory Deprivation

Whereas drugs may be necessary for some, conditions of limited sensory stimulation may work for others. Experimental sensory deprivation can be total dark isolation without tactile sensation in a soundproof room or immersion in a tank of water. Ganzfeld conditions are less extreme and provide homogenous visual and auditory sensation to a person in a relaxed position. As sensory input is decreased in these situations or as in meditation or hypnosis, motor output is decreased. As the motor system shuts down, one seems to disidentify with it to some extent. If it is not in full operation, it does not need one's complete attention. At these times, one may be able to turn attention to different states of being. One of these possible states may be an experience of being distant from the sensorimotor system which we call our body.

Spencer Sherman of the Maryland Psychiatric Research Center worked with people in very deep hypnosis who were reporting OBES. He felt they progressively experienced and then "turned off" (in order to go still deeper into hypnosis) more and more basic conscious functions. At the most profound depths, the hypnotized individual had succeeded in turning off almost all conscious activity and what was left was the awareness of pure "being," through which the person felt identical to everything in the universe.

As an experimental idea, it may be interesting to place two people in hypnosis, without knowledge of the other, and have each project to a certain predetermined location and report what they see. Would they be able to give details of the place where they had never been before? More important, would they see each other there?

Relaxation and Meditative Practices

Some people find that relaxation exercises, mental concentration, or meditation practices may be the only stimulus needed for a first projection; OBES may be a surprising result of such deliberate practices. One may be expecting enlightenment, but not necessarily weightlessness. Philosophical reflections on the question of personal identity may also initiate an OBE or take place during the experience. Celia Green[2] found from her psychological analyses that a common if not crucial feature of OBES is freedom from emotional conflict. Therefore, just being in a state where one's mind is blank can sometimes precipitate an OBE.

A person may become rather numb during these exercises and the lack of muscle signals may be enough to convince the person that he or she is no longer physically in contact with the body. About a third of the people who reported OBES in Celia Green's studies stated that there was less muscle tone or more muscular relaxation during the experiences.

Since many experiences are brought about by stress conditions, it is difficult to understand the frequency of these statements about relaxation. It could be that under stress, people get less than adequate muscular feedback to the brain to form an opinion as to their degree of muscle tone. A state of semiparalysis due to shock may be misinterpreted as relaxed muscles. This type of misinformation occurs in other situations, for example a paralyzed limb may not feel as if it belongs to the body. On the other hand, an amputated limb may be experienced and felt as if it still was there and belonged to the body. Neurons in the brain which correspond to missing limbs seem to have to die out through lack of use in order for the memory and sensation of the limb to be extinguished.

Findings in psychomotor epilepsy suggest that as the epileptic gets less and less accurate bodily and muscle signals to the brain, or the interpretation of such information is distorted, a situation is created in which one is unable to identify with and remember what is going on in the external environment, including one's own body. This same sort of withdrawing conscious control from body parts through progressive relaxation or meditation may produce a similar effect.

Regardless of the circumstances which provide the impetus for an OBE, people often remark that on leaving the body and then looking back at it, it appeared to be relaxed.

Life-Threatening Situations

Accidents. Automobile accidents are the stimuli for some first spontaneous OBES. The fact that you are physically tossed about in such a circumstance may account for the belief that one is actually loose from one's body. The body may only be propelled through the windshield and onto the top of the hood, but the perceptive consciousness may experience itself as up about as high as telephone lines looking down on the calamity with cool detachment and no pain. Near-drowning incidents sometimes result in people having panoramic views of their lives, but occasionally when one is going down for the third time, the experience is perceived from above where there is an abundance of life-sustaining air.

Falls. There are many stories of mountaineers who experienced OBES during dangerous falls. Zurich geology professor Albert Heim collected anecdotes from climbers and other people who had experienced near-fatal falls. His findings were published around the turn of the century in the Yearbook of the Swiss Alpine Club.[3]

Unconsciousness or Coma. One may find awareness out of alignment with the body on regaining consciousness after an accident. Concussion patients, as well as those who have been anesthetized during operations, may wake up in an out-of-body condition. People have reported rather long and involved OBES as having occurred during coma states.

Operations. Many spontaneous OBES occur when a patient is on the operating table under anesthesia. These patients report that they were totally aware during the operation, and that they consciously watched procedures from a distance. They can even sometimes repeat remarks of doctors and nurses spoken during the operation. They report being in full possession of their senses and able to move about.

There have also been reports in the literature of doctors who saw phantom forms rising above unconscious patients on the operating table. Others have reported seeing doubles of comatose patients walking around the sick room seemingly in perfect health.

Near-Death Experiences. There are numerous reports of patients who have been declared "clinically dead" who have lived to tell of their experiences during this critical time. With no vital signs of respiration, heartbeat, or brain-wave activity, these patients have apparently been able to watch resuscitation attempts and later report the actions of those present, to their astonishment. A patient in near-fatal circumstances may have other types of experiences and visions but when they can give verifiable information of activities taking place while they were believed to be dead, the evidence for some objective OBE is hard to refute.

Prolonged Illness. Many OBES are instantaneous or last only a few seconds or a few moments. However, in a prolonged illness, a person may experience being distant from the body for days or even months. Patients in such a state have difficulty understanding why nurses or doctors, whom they see and speak to, cannot hear them. Such a prolonged OBE may come about as a result of a high fever which will not yield to treatment.

Psychological Stress

Physical stress, such as that experienced in accidents or illness, is not the only stress factor in OBES. Terror may cause one to instantaneously project to a safe distance. Extreme fear of possible pain or death may be the stimulus for an OBE. Soldiers hearing shells falling all around them and civilians in air raids have reported OBES under this kind of stress.

Job pressures or working under any continuous anxiety or strain may bring about recurrent OBES, wherein one might observe oneself working from a distance. These people may not experience OBES at any other time in their lives.

Psychotic patients who experience mental stress by reason of not being able to filter out unmanageable over-loads of exogenous or endogenous stimuli (stimuli from outside or inside one's body) may find relief in releasing themselves temporarily from the overwhelming conditions. If fear barriers keep us "in the body," then a lack of psychological defenses might encourage escape. It is important to remember that there is escape "to" as well as escape "from." During psychotic episodes, one may be able to retain a modicum of mental health under extreme pressure only be escaping to a safer place until the psychological trauma is over.

Patients who report autoscopic experiences (seeing one's double in space) are often prone to deliberate, selfconscious self-observation. There seems to be a tendency for the ego to split into acting and observing fragments. Self-observations range from sensations to feelings of observing oneself as an object. In the presence of pain, physical or mental, the ego may try to save itself by splitting off the fragment felt to be the source of pain and projecting it away from the body.

If one has an unfulfilled need or desire, an OBE may resolve the frustration. For instance, you may have a strong need or desire to see a loved one. Either party may be in a dangerous or crisis situation. This is not necessary to precipitate an OBE to a loved one, but it is fairly common in reports. In one case, a sick mother who could not get out of bed desired to see her newborn, who was out of visual range in another room. She reportedly removed her point of view to the room where her child was located.

Learning Exercise

Sandor B. Brent[4] is interested in OBES that occur in ordinary, noncrisis, nonmystical contexts. He is a developmental psychologist who had induced OBES as a learning exercise in college students for over ten years. He originally devised his technique to aid in sensitivity training and to teach participants that they are not merely passive recipients of their conscious experiences, but are active agents in the construction of these experiences. He proposes that we create objective reality, as well as our own experience of our bodies, with our minds.

His technique is extremely interesting and is reported as being effective with widely varying groups of individuals. The method is clearly described and therefore subject to controlled research and replication. One change needed in the process might be to culminate the projection in a verifiable location rather than in outer space where Brent eventually leads his participants. A trip to outer space is probably more fascinating for the students, but too subjective to obtain empirical evidence. Indeed, participants often question whether what they experienced in the induced OBE was "just imagination."

Spirit Possession

If certain states are conducive to one's experience of getting out of the body, what states might facilitate the feeling that someone or something else has been getting into one's body? Religions throughout the world that practice spirit possession as part of their ritual give us some clues.

"Falling to the drums" during religious ceremonies is by far the most common immediate stimulus for possession. Singing, clapping, or any rhythmic beating of gongs or rattles are also effective in creating an altered state of consciousness within the group. Strong emotion, such as fear, rage, grief, awe, or wonder, may help precipitate trance possession.

Those who already feel possessed by some spirit may approach bystanders and anoint them or simply rub their heads, chests, faces, and arms to bring them also into a state of possession. Leaders may pick people up and hold them in the air or spin them around by the waist and thereby induce possession.

Members of the group who hope to be possessed on a special occasion usually fast. Even one day without food with this expectant attitude may provide the first occasion of possession. The resultant low level of blood sugar from the fast may facilitate dissociation.

Whereas expectation of a possession state is sometimes important, at other times a personal crisis may be an important stimulus. Those confronted by serious family or other interpersonal problems, difficult decisions, personal loss, involvement in court cases, or other major frustrating or conflict-producing events may fall into possession more easily than those at peace. An OBE may also sometimes be seen as an escape from traumatic situations. Those who are ostracized by society may find some kind of acceptance through both types of experiences, as well.

End Notes

[1]Sylvan Muldoon and Hereward Carrington, *The Projection of the Astral Body* (New York: Weiser, n.d.), pp. 34-36.

[2]Celia Green, *Out of the Body Experiences* (New York: Ballantine, 1973). This study is based on the results of 326 questionnaires returned through a British radio and press appeal. It is a psychological study of the characteristics of personal OBES. Reprinted in paperback.

[3]*Schweizer Alpenclub Jahrbuch* (Bern, Switzerland: 1864-1924).

[4]Sandor B. Brent, "Deliberately Induced, Premortem, Out-of-Body Experiences: An Experimental and Theoretical Approach," in *Between Life and Death*, ed. Robert Kastenbaum (New York: Springer Publishing Co., 1979), pp. 89-123.

Chapter III

Other Authorities:
Those Who Do It

Most literature on out-of-body experiences mentions the personal experimentation of four men: Yram, Fox, Muldoon, and Whiteman. They will also be considered in this chapter, but first let's look at projectors who are doing their own experiments today. In order to understand how they are approaching this phenomenon, we will look at their different techniques, ideas, and uses of OBE. We will also need to discuss the writings of two women, which preceded Muldoon's publication in America.

D. Scott Rogo has been personally experimenting, thinking, and writing about OBES since the 1960s. He actually achieved projections from 1965 to 1967. From 1967 to 1970, he went away from his home to attend college and this put a stop to his OBES. He has had them occasionally since 1970 and had several in 1977, in which he was aware of being in his own home while he was actually 3,000 miles away.[1]

When Rogo first started to experiment with OBE, he had no success trying the mental techniques of Fox or Muldoon. He then read Preston Hall's article, "Experiments in Astral Projection,"[2] and discovered a dietary regime which he felt would be helpful in producing an OBE. He dieted on fruit and vegetables, carrots in particular, and small amounts of meat. He could not eat the raw eggs Hall recommended. After only two weeks of this diet, in a moment of extreme exhaustion, lying on his bed, he became aware of a physical rigidity with pulsating and falling sensations and knew a projection might be taking place. He concentrated on the feeling of falling and soon found himself staring at his own body. He moved about the room somewhat before blacking out and then awakening back in his body.

21

A few weeks later he had a similar experience in which he was able to gain enough control to pass through his closed bedroom door in a standing position and go into his living room. When he found himself back in his body, he was satisfied that a person could move out of the body with perception, decision-making abilities, and some conscious control of the experience.

After achieving this experiential goal, he stopped experimenting and stopped Hall's diet. However, his OBES continued for the next two years and he was able to devise a system for bringing them about. Whatever barriers had kept him "in the body" prior to these first two experiences had been transcended and his confinement to seeing from only his physical eyes was ended.

He was usually surprised to find himself out of body in his spontaneous experiences, but Rogo writes that he felt really frightened only a couple of times. Once he became afraid when he "saw several white faces to the side of me," and once when he felt he was being pulled out through his head against his will. Other personal experimenters have recounted numerous frightening experiences and they repeatedly warn novices to beware. Rogo usually reports earthly experiences so it is possible he did not venture into more unknown and dangerous environs and conditions.

Since most of his OBES occurred just before going to sleep, he knew that this period of relaxation filled with mental imagery (called the hypnagogic state) was most important. Just as Fox and others manipulated lucid dreams to gain OBES, Rogo managed some control over these hypnagogic images. His method is straightforward: become aware of your imagery just before entering sleep, learn to maintain a panoramic view of the images, and try to extend and control the images with your purpose in mind.

For instance, while lying awake Rogo saw himself driving a car. He consciously decided to drive the car off the road and crash it in the image. He felt that when the car crashed, he would be projected out of his body. This method worked on his first attempt and he used it repeatedly to bring about OBES. A "driving image" worked for him, but others may find that falling, flying, swinging, or surfing images are most related to their OBES. Individuals who want to try this technique must discover for themselves which image feels right and then practice shifting from imagery to OBE rather than to sleep or the waking state.

Rogo has done a most extensive research of OBE literature and in 1978 he edited a fine book covering many aspects of the experience. It is entitled *Mind Beyond the Body*[3] and is must reading for anyone who is seriously thinking about OBEs.

Another contemporary who wrote a book about his personal experiments is Robert Monroe. His book, *Journeys Out of the Body*,[4] lacks sufficient verification to make his experiences real to me, but I suppose if I could duplicate his feats, that would be proof enough. A lot of his experiences took place in what he calls "Locale II," a nonmaterial environment with laws of motion and matter only remotely related to the physical world. It would seem wise to thoroughly validate one's experiences on this earth — Locale I — before concentrating on other-worldly experiences.

Today, many personal experimenters seem to concentrate on earthly OBEs rather than those which make great stories but are impossible to verify. It is difficult to imagine the kind of environment Monroe reports: a place where there is no time; where thought produces energy that can be transformed into material form; where thought provides instantaneous communication and perception. If this is the *natural* environment of the Second Body, as Monroe suggests, and if one goes forth into this space with "no hiding layers of conditioning or inhibition [to] shield the inner you from others, where honesty is the best policy because there can be nothing less," I wonder how many of us are ready to make this trip.

A successful, middle-aged businessman, Monroe began to feel strange physical vibrations in 1958 and several months after the onset of these sensations, he had his first partial OBE. He extended his sense of touch from his hand (hanging over the side of his bed) down through the floor and ended up touching some water. There are two accounts of this story in print. In one, it seems he was on the second floor of a building and in the other on the first floor. A book by Harold Sherman, *Your Mysterious Powers of ESP*,[5] contained an interview with "Robert Penn" (a pseudonym for Monroe) and the above experience here is described as vibratory sensations and then finding himself bumping against the ceiling. These kinds of discrepancies in reporting tend, perhaps unfairly, to make one skeptical of Monroe's veracity.

In 1966, Monroe had some limited, mixed success in only one of nine experimental sessions with Charles Tart, then at the University of Virginia, but most of his reported experiences lie outside the realm of critical objective analysis. When I last saw him in October 1972 he looked pale and debilitated and he had been advised to decrease his OBE experimenting. He mentioned some characteristics of his experiences at that time:

> During OBE his vision is somewhat distorted and myopic but he says he can see in all directions at once. He thinks if we can learn how the vision works, it will give us clues to the energy involved.
>
> He thinks a dynamic target, such as another person, should work best in experimenting. He feels it is easier to go to a person than a place.
>
> When he reenters his body, first he gets into physical proximity and then sort of slides in from the bottom.
>
> He had not had the sense of taste or smell during an OBE.
>
> His experiences were not spontaneous, but were the results of a deliberate process.
>
> He found, as Fox had, that intense emotion seems to put the brakes on an experience.
>
> He felt alcohol depressed his experience and that Vitamin C enhanced it. Other dietary changes had no effect on the experience.

Alex Tanous, born November 26, 1926, in Maine, has cooperated in the OBE work at the American Society for Psychical Research since 1973. Some scientific data have been published on his results and the mere fact that parapsychologists continue to work with him on a monthly basis indicates that they are quite satisfied with his efforts. His OBES in daily life do seem to produce striking results. People from all across the country contact him to find missing persons and lost objects, locate silver mines and other natural resources, and solve police cases. He is often successful in these endeavors.

He experienced his first OBES as a child and has continued to study and use them over the years. The practicality of his OBES is most impressive. He moves about in space and time and once he relived the scene of a crime to such an extent that he was able to draw a facial sketch of a murderer which matched up with a composite picture Canadian authorities had drawn.

People have reported seeing him when he is miles away. When his apparition is seen, he has no recollection of being there even though he may have thought of the person who saw him at the time of the report. He claims many psychic abilities in his autobiography[6] which are often overlapping, but his love of OBES is attested to by his consistent work on the phenomenon for the past seven years at the ASPR.

Several men and women left written accounts of their OBES in the early twentieth century. The stories presented by two of the men, Muldoon and Fox, seem to have received more credibility in subsequent literature although all reports were of a subjective nature. Two women, however, had books published on their OBES before either of these men.

The Rev. Cora L.V. Richmond was a spiritualist minister born in 1840 near Cuba, New York. Harrison D. Barrett has supplied us with a book of her life work.[7] She died in 1923. At the end of Barrett's book, Richmond reports many experiences out of her body in which she visited others on earth and communicated with them. Her spiritual experiences started at age 11 and continued throughout her life. As a "control medium," she taught from England to California from her early teens.

In her own book, *My Experiences While Out of My Body*,[8] she hints of a severe illness that lasted for several months. During her illness she had a "prolonged visit to the spirit states." Her OBE was totally involved with spirit guides, angels, and others existing in beautiful surroundings where they taught and helped other spirits and human beings toward more evolved states of being and awareness.

She appears also to have been somewhat political and she gave talks on diversified topics. One discourse in Chicago in 1886 was attributed to her body's having been temporarily possessed by Wendell Phillips, who spoke through her. The positions taken were abolitionist, prohibitionist, and pro labor.

Caroline D. Larsen had her first spontaneous OBE in Vermont in 1910. At first her experiences were "confined to the limits of my home.... For some unknown reason [by] a woman spirit." She gradually extended her trips until she was free to travel wherever she desired. Her spirit body felt substantial and was a duplicate of her physical body. She experienced all five senses, but more intensely than in her normal physical condition.

She soon felt that she was communicating with spirits of the deceased who lingered on earth without the realization that they had lost their bodies. Her descriptions of various planes of spirit coincide to some degree with the reports of the Rev. Richmond.

In contrast to reports from Yram of radioactive waves and electromagnetic energies (described below), these two women report visions of tremendous lights and colors, of helpers ever ready to aid, and feelings of love, joy, and peace. Whereas astral romance is absent from both records, Larsen perceived that masculine and feminine were sharply defined in the Spirit World. "[M]en were in authority, but this gave them no actual dominion over women, for both take their proper places, and both have their missions. The work of the men is more creative; women conserve and apply. Men are administrators; women inspire to beauty and sweetness, and are angels of mercy, comforters, teachers, and mother spirits.... The modesty and grace of women is set over against the strength and authority of men."[9]

Yram was born Marcel Louis Forhan on November 17, 1884, in Corbell, France, and died at the age of 33 in China. He wrote several mystical volumes, but most have not been translated. One book in translation, *Practical Astral Projection*,[10] seems far from stressing practicality. Approximately 85 percent of the book contains metaphysical theories which Yram evolved during his personal experimentation.

He lists essential conditions for the experience as good mental and physical health, moderation in all things, a peaceful life, and, above all, a noble ideal as your goal. Many of the experiences he describes were on other levels of existence than earth. He believes we have a series of bodies of different densities and dimensions all under the power of our conscious will and that, therefore, calm self-control is an absolute necessity. His interactions with matter, for example, going through substances such as walls or not being able to do so, depended on the density of the body he was operating through at that particular time.

We read of astral romance in many stories of OBES, but Yram's story is too good to omit. Yram paid periodic astral visits to the woman who later became his wife. She was able to feel his presence and some sort of telepathic communication occurred to such an extent that Yram states they even became engaged during one of these visits. After marriage, they would often travel together in space. He tells of one experience where their subtle bodies interpenetrated each other in a most intimate and ecstatic spiritual union.

There is a lot of talk in his book about electromagnetism, radioactive waves, centrifugal and centripetal forces, and various strata of energy and ether. He believes that OBES are available to even the most skeptical, that they can be studied and explained scientifically, and that "To suppose that I have been able to imagine all the details of the experiences I have related would be to endow me with qualities far more perfect than those needed in order to project the astral body" (pages 248-249).

Sylvan Muldoon, like so many self-projectionists, had an early OBE (at age 12). It was during a visit to a spiritualist camp in the Midwest with his mother. Whereas Yram states that good mental and physical health are essential, Muldoon was the antithesis of this ideal. He was a frail young man with many ailments confining him to bed for long periods of time. As Muldoon became healthier, his OBES became less frequent and all but disappeared. Another refutation of Yram's theory comes from Vincent Turvey, an invalid, who recorded many of his projections in his book *Beginnings of Seership*.[11] From the many spontaneous reports available, it would seem that what works perfectly for one experient is totally inadequate for another. Individuals using completely opposite systems are able to achieve comparable results in self-projection.

Muldoon was interested in astral projection for approximately 35 years from 1915 to 1950. He started communicating with Hereward Carrington around 1927 and in 1929 their first book on the subject was published.[12] This is the most explicit book available on actual techniques and it is entitled *The Projection of the Astral Body*. Many theories and practical suggestions are discussed in detail.

For instance, Muldoon felt that falling and flying dreams may be due to actual movements of the astral body (Monroe later also adopted this point of view). Flying dreams often preceded Muldoon's OBES. He believed he could move objects while projected from a dream but not while projected from a waking state.

One interesting experiment Muldoon tried was to touch his physical body while exterior to it. He was unable to do so. He always tried to verify his experiences to the best of his ability and his written descriptions have been reprinted several times since 1929. His astral body was an exact duplicate of his physical body and all his projections were within earth's environs. His mother, as well as his lover, saw his phantom on several occasions.

He reported feeling physical pain at times while out of his body. This is somewhat unusual since many spontaneous projections due to accidents produce a sense of release from pain in the victim. One time he reports coming back into his body to find it paralyzed, speechless, and twitching for about three minutes. Can you imagine the horror of such an experience? But, Muldoon kept right on experimenting. Whereas he noted some of the dangers of OBE, he did not urge others not to try projection but tried to teach them how to do it successfully. Since he himself felt free to experiment; he felt it was everyone's right.

He believes there is a definite advantage in fasting, while trying to promote projection. His theory on fasting is that the astral body moves out of the physical during sleep in order to recharge with cosmic energy. Food, along with sleep and breathing, are three energy sources. When food is omitted as in fasting, the astral has to move further out of the physical during sleep to gather extra energy in order to compensate, according to Muldoon.

He states that the second body can be projected in a conscious or unconscious state, so it is quite possible people are doing this often but not realizing it. He gives detailed descriptions of techniques of self-projection, such as dream control, intentional desire for motivation, projecting to familiar places, slowing the heart (he warns those with heart disease not to attempt these experiments), and self-observation.

Whereas Muldoon never ventured off into "higher realms," he did experience encounters with other disembodied entities during some projections. He concluded that immortality was a solid fact — and somewhat of a burden. He seems to have lost interest in the subject after 1950 and he died in Wisconsin in 1971.

Oliver Fox was born Hugh G. Callaway on November 30, 1885, in Southampton, England. In retrospect, he considered himself a delicate, highly strung, temperamental child with many illnesses. His dearly beloved mother died when he was 13 and his father died six months later. He tried to communicate with his mother for over 40 years but received only one rather obscure message, assumed to be from her, which came through his own automatic writing.

His experiments extended from 1902 to 1938. At first they were confined to this world and he used a lucid dream technique to get out. He called it the "Dream of Knowledge," wherein he would try to keep his critical faculty awake while he physically went to sleep and then to discern any discrepancy in a scene so that he might realize he was dreaming. During projection, if he felt a pain in his head, he would at first immediately return to his body. But one time he stayed out, endured the intense pain, and something seemed to "click" in his brain. He was then free to go anywhere he wanted. It wasn't long before he was soaring through space and having unimaginable adventures. Fox would sometimes become so emotionally involved in his OBES that the intensity of his emotions would abruptly terminate them.

Fox believed he had a soul and left his body many times with full consciousness of his duality. He became even more convinced of OBES when his lover projected herself to his room one night and made her presence known to him. The next day she described his room in detail. One of the details she described was unknown to him and he later verified it. He was positive she had never seen his room in person.

Fox warns would-be projectors of many dangers, including heart failure, insanity, cerebral hemorrhage, and premature burial. He then adds: "Very likely these experiments are not more dangerous than motoring; but I must confess that I do not really understand what I have been doing."[13]

Dr. J.H.M. Whiteman considered his OBES only as steps toward the highest mystical experience of all, Deificatio. This experience seems comparable to what Yram called Unity/Multiplicity. A very simplified definition might be an experience where one realizes that "everything is everything" and "I am that."

Whiteman's book, *The Mystical Life*, is mystifying indeed. As a philosopher, his terminology is abstract and difficult to comprehend. The book contains descriptions and analyses of his own mystical experiences over a period of 50 years. At age 12 (1919), Whiteman experienced a full separation of his consciousness from his body, which he did not recognize as such at the time. He was able to achieve partial and full separations for 30 years before publishing his experiences. He recorded approximately two full separations per month for 22 years following June 1931. Over 2,000 experiences of varying degrees were recorded by him during this period. Four experiences were classified as Mystical Form Liberation but detailed records of this type could not be found.

From his earliest memories he suffered the mental

anguish of those who feel they do not quite fit in their physical bodies. His questions concerning one's spiritual sex, if any, were resolved in 1953. He writes, "... with me the presence of the Source and the knowledge of being feminine in heart-disposition and intelligible form go so absolutely together that the one without the other is impossible.... [T]o forget the intelligible femininity for one moment is to forget the Source, and therefore to succumb to a spiritual death" (page 230). During separation he sometimes experienced himself as female in form and once expressed "the heartfelt thought, 'I am so glad I am a girl'." He felt this was his proper nature and experienced an intense sense of joy "that that proper nature should be so absolutely what I could most wish for myself, both in general and in every possible particular" (page 200). In intelligible form, much like Plato's Ideal, he felt himself to be feminine. He studied his astral form in detail, which reminds one of autoscopy (seeing one's double), and he sometimes found himself in a child's body (age 2 to 17).

One of his chief interests seems to be to explain why the human form representative of the mind in a separated state differs from one's physical body. Though he studied OBEs for 50 years, Whiteman states, "... much of the experience was so tremendous in its import as to be far beyond explanation" (page 13).

End Notes

[1]D. Scott Rogo, "A Haunting by a Living Agent," *Theta* 6 (nos. 2 & 3) (1978):15-20.

[2]Preston Hall, "Experiments in Astral Projection," *Journal of the American Society for Psychical Research* 22 (1918):39-60.

[3]D. Scott Rogo, *Mind Beyond the Body* (New York: Penguin, 1978). Paperback anthology of the best experimental and theoretical work done on OBEs to date.

[4]Robert A. Monroe, *Journeys Out of the Body* (New York: Doubleday, 1971). Subjective account of his OBEs.

[5]Harold Sherman, *Your Mysterious Powers of ESP* (New York: New American Library, 1969), pp. 189-199. Contains personal cases reported to Sherman over the years and some of his thoughts concerning OBEs. Interesting and easy to read.

[6]Alex Tanous and Harvey Ardman, *Beyond Coincidence* (New York: Doubleday, 1976), pp. 113-147. Personal account of his research at the ASPR.

[7]H.D. Barrett, *Life Work of Cora L.V. Richmond* (Chicago: Hack & Anderson, 1895), pp. 725-729.

[8]Cora L.V. Richmond, *My Experiences While Out of My Body* (Boston: Christopher Publishing House, 1923).

[9]Caroline D. Larsen, *My Travels in the Spirit World* (Rutland, Vt.: Tuttle, 1927), pp. 99-100. Personally published, subjective account of her experiences in other existences.

[10]Yram, *Practical Astral Projection* (New York: Weiser, 1974). Personal record of his experiences, reprinted and in paperback.

[11]Vincent Turvey, *The Beginnings of Seership: Astral Projection, Clairvoyance and Prophecy* (New Hyde Park, N.Y.: University Books, 1969).

[12]Sylvan Muldoon and H. Carrington, *The Projection of the Astral Body* (New York: Weisner, n.d.). Autobiographical. Includes diagrams and descriptions of his theories. Reprinted in paperback.

[13]Oliver Fox, *Astral Projection* (New Hyde Park, N.Y.: University Books, 1962). Records of personal OBEs and experimentation. As one of the first people to write up experiences and discuss them, this book is a classic and has been reprinted in paperback.

[14]J.H.M. Whiteman, *The Mystical Life* (London: Faber & Faber, 1961). Personal accounts of OBEs. Philosophical and scholarly.

Chapter IV
How Long Has This Been Going On?

Thousands of reports over the ages from people, who have had the experience of perceiving from a point of view different from their physical eyes, cannot be brushed aside nonchalantly. Can it all be malobservation or irrationality, or can one actually operate independently from a body? Anecdotal evidence is not conclusive, but the mere bulk of this kind of data compels researchers to try to answer this essential question of personal existence. Therefore, as you will see in the next chapter, some scientists continue to investigate the possibility of out-of-body experiences.

The belief that we are immortal spirits is the basis of all religions. Philosophy, creed, terminology, and practical application of one's faith differ but two concepts that religionists have in common are that we are spiritual beings and live after our bodies are destroyed.

There is evidence that Egyptians believed in the *Ka*, which corresponds to later concepts of an astral body. The *Ka* was not the soul itself, but a vehicle of the mind and soul. The most important religious writing of the Egyptians, the *Papyrus of Ani*, contains hieroglyphics that have been interpreted as stating: "Let my Ba-soul come forth to walk about here and there and wherever it pleases." Parts of this scroll were created as early as 5000 B.C. *The Book of the Dead*, which is a translation of the *Papyrus of Ani*, states that "the Ba-soul inhabited the Ka, or double."

Initiations into the Egyptian mysteries of Isis and Osiris are reported to have included techniques to enable projection so that the initiate might have proof of survival of bodily death. Many ancient rituals, initiation rites, myths, and legends address themselves to the desire of human beings to act like spirits, to operate as spirit.

From ancient Greek papyri, it has been ascertained that initiation rites of Mithraism contained elements of earlier Minoan religion. The whole Mithra-cult rite is concentrated on bringing to birth the perfected subtle body of the initiate. This idea seems to have been appealing to individuals for thousands of years. Freedom and transcendence of ordinary daily life are sought in thoughts of heavenly ascent, descent to the underworld, magical flight, and invisibility.

This desire to realize one's nonphysical nature is expressed in initiation rites across cultures through mystical death and rebirth, dismemberment of the body, and strengthening of the memory. Early peoples understood that it is not enough to attain ecstatic experience, but one must remember it. A lack of memory may be the reason most OBEs today are unconsciously forgotten, if not consciously invalidated or suppressed. Symbolic dismemberment of the body and restoration are enacted so that the initiate can become a spiritual body with clear sight and understanding, immortality, and immunity from natural limitations. Mystical death and rebirth ceremonies have the same purpose.

The Tibetan Book of the Dead resembles the Egyptian *Book of the Dead* sufficiently to suggest some cultural relationship between the two. The Tibetan manual embodies A.D. 700s teachings concerning death of the physical body and experiences encountered thereafter. The *Bardo-body* is described as a state in which the deceased find themselves.

> The Bardo body, formed of matter in an invisible or ethereal-like state, is an exact duplicate of the human body, from which it is separated in the process of death. Retained in the Bardo body are the consciousness-principle and the psychic nerve system (the counterpart ... of the physical nerve system of the human body).[1]

The Bardo-body is said to have supernormal faculties which one begins to make use of much as a newborn learns to use its sense faculties.[2]

Mahayana Buddhism allies itself with Tibetan Buddhism and contains the doctrine of Kayatraya—the principle of three bodies. Buddha is reported as answering a disciple's question concerning this doctrine that there are "three bodies; the body of the law, the body of perfect enjoyment, the apparitional body." Tibetan literature states that the mother of Buddha prior to his birth experienced an out-of-body state. D. Scott Rogo[3] gives source material for the many reports of Buddha and his disciples' transcending time and space.

Yogis claim powers to transcend bodies but stress, in for example *The Yoga Aphorisms of Patanjali,* that these powers are the greatest stumbling blocks in the path of truth if not viewed correctly. Focusing on the miracle of psychic phenomena itself obscures the eternal principal behind it, that is, that we are immortal spirits moving through time, space, and matter. There are instructions for withdrawing the mind from the body through meditative techniques, but these powers are to be obtained for the knowledge of one's nonphysical existence and then they are to be given up in order that one can experience true liberation.

Different civilizations have given many names to the entity suspected of leaving the body during life in an OBE and at death. Beliefs in multiple souls or nonphysical aspects are common, the numbers usually being two, three, or four. However, some tribes envisage thirty or forty individual aspects in each human being. The second body principle of the Hindus is called Pranamayakosha and the spirit within is referred to as *Atman.* In Buddhism, the realization of one's Buddha nature is sought, but another name for the free spirit is *rupa.* The ancient Chinese meditated to achieve OBE and believed that the second body resided in the solar plexus and was released by action of the spirit. The double, called *thankhi,* leaving the body through the head, and other out-of-body processes familiar to students of astral projection were depicted on seventeenth-century wooden tablets. Chinese philosophers believed in a seven-fold nature of humans, that is, that each person experiences seven different levels of existence (whether they are aware of it or not).

Ancient Kabalistic doctrine describes the soul as being suspended from body and attached via a cord at the larynx. Hebrews referred to the spirit as *raukh* and the soul as *nephesch.* For them, the word *pneuma* meant something material. Greek-speaking Jews, however, later translated *raukh* to *pneuma* and *nephesch* to *psyche.* Other Greek-speaking Semites also used *pneuma* to translate the word in their languages that corresponded to the Hebrew *raukh.* Some Greeks used the word *eidolon* to designate a discarnate entity. Hellenized Semites referred to personal beings without bodies, whether nonhuman beings, angels, devils or human spirits, as *pneumata*. Plotinus and the neoplatonists adopted the word *nous* and it was translated by early Christians as spirit.

For Aristotle, consciousness could only exist within a body and was distributed over the whole body, not localized in the head or any other body part. Plato, on the other hand, allows that a soul can take leave of a body and travel in a visual space without being centered in any one particular place. This space, which has no circumference, is the domain of platonic ideals, the realm of the pure, eternal and immortal, the domain of intelligible archetypes, which are painless, divine, immanent, simple, and indestructible. The idea of such a transfer of the properties of the soul, including perception and intellect, to cosmic space did not originate with Plato but was inherited from earlier Greek Pythagorean and Orphic beliefs in the separation of an immortal soul from a body, which represented a prison or tomb. There are written records or experiences, which resemble OBES, by both Socrates and Plotinus. Plutarch, in *On the Delay of Divine Justice*, gives an account of an OBE of Aridaeus of Asia Minor in A.D. 79.

In Europe, Romans used the term *larva* for the inner nonmaterial life. Pre-Germanic tribes held a theory of six body elements. Of these, *litr* was a very fine substance that connected the physical body to the senses. Norwegians sometimes called the out-of-body entity *fylgje*, but more often they called it the *vardøgr*.

Perceiving the apparition of a living person was so prevalent in Germany that the term for this second image, *Doppelgänger*, became an English word. This phenomenon, as well as the Norwegian *vardøgr*, takes the form of a "forerunner," that is, a phantom of a person is seen shortly before the body appears. In these cases, the phantom has no consciousness and the person is unaware this is happening, even though the double is substantial enough to be seen by others. A fundamental question, one yet to be adequately answered, could be explored by analyzing detailed reports of spontaneous cases of this type. It would be interesting to ascertain the temporal sequence between appearance of the double and arrival of the person at the same location.

The ancient Britons had many names for the out-of-body entity, including *fetch, waft, task,* and *fye.* In the highlands and islands of Scotland, J.G. Campbell collected several stories of people who saw and were sometimes haunted by "spectres of the living" called *tamhasg.* These doubles were believed to be external realities having an existence of their own.

Western mystics, including Quaker ministers, Mormon preachers, and Roman Catholic saints have claimed the ability to leave their bodies. St. Teresa of Avila's autobiography contains descriptions of her ecstacies and she writes that at times "one feels one has been transported into another and different region. The soul is suspended in such a way that it seems to be completely outside itself."

Present-day shamans in non-Western cultures, including Siberia, usually report being able to leave their bodies in order to do their work more efficiently. They often seem to "possess spirits," whereas followers are more often perceived as being "possessed by spirits." Australian aborigines claim that their "clever men" can project themselves out of their bodies at will. Géza Róheim investigated the beliefs and religious customs of the Aranda tribes of Central Australia. These people believe in a double (*ngancha*) which is just like the real man and which is considered to be the source of life.

Ideas about the spiritual life of women differ radically from that of men in many societies. For instance, in the Aranda tribe women do not possess a *ngancha* themselves but in their dreams they see a man's double as a demon always chasing them with an enormous penis. Róheim seems convinced that, for the Aranda, the double is a personification of the phallus.

Historically, female initiation rites have centered around sexuality rather than spirituality. Women do not focus during initiation on freedom and transcendence; their purpose is revelation that the female initiate is a creator of life. Females often behave immodestly during initiation to symbolically abolish societal norms of daily living, but the idea of woman's being a free spirit is not conveyed. Spinning and weaving are taught and performed to reinforce her idea of herself as creator.

Ideas on the nonphysical nature of humans are fraught with geographical and cultural differences concerning male and female, names, theories, elements, and also concepts. For instance, many American Indians think the soul is a manikin. Malays believe the soul to be no bigger than a thumb. Some natives of the Congo believe the soul resides in the blood (if you lose enough blood, you die). Some think it is in the heart because the heart pounds when you are excited and stops when you die. The liver is a favorite location for the soul; the Macusi say the soul is "the man in our eyes" (globally more favored than the head).

Europeans' beliefs that your soul is in your reflection in a mirror causes them to turn mirrors to the wall when one is sick lest the soul be overexposed. Some societies believe that photographs, like reflections, may contain a part of one's soul. Many think the soul is in the breath. Even before the dualistic concept of the double, G.R.S. Mead[4] conjectures that "in the [cultural] beginnings the soul was apparently believed to be air, and air breath, and breath spirit, and spirit and soul one...." It was only later that the human soul was considered "a rational reality or activity, an intelligible life, an immaterial essence, and not body or an embodiment or element of any kind." Language more often associates the words breath or wind with spirit than with soul. Superstitions emerged from these ideas so that people were careful to cover their mouths when they yawned, lest the soul escape. Some intellectual suppositions appeared in a book review in *Science* magazine in 1899:

> It is, in fact, certain that very many forms of disease, known as anaemia, neurasthenia, echolalia and the like are due to temporary absence of the posthom shadow [i.e., double].[5]

In the United States in the 1960s, a follower of Father Divine told me how once, alone in his room, his heart began to pound and he thought he was having a heart attack or stroke. He called for Father Divine, whose double immediately appeared, gave him breathing instructions, and helped him safely through the frightening experience. Should we assume this was only a fantasy? Have we a right to deny that there are those who can invisibly roam about and help and heal those who are alone and in trouble? I could hardly deny the gentleman's story about Father Divine because for a man in his seventies, he looked and felt great, and was having a joyous life experience full of gratitude and love. To try to shake that kind of faith would be unforgiveably arrogant. Unfortunately, it is not unusual for people to invalidate experiences that they have not had personally.

The anthropologist Sir E.B. Tylor, in his book *Primitive Culture*, attributes reports of OBEs and beliefs about them to fantasy and dreaming. It is difficult to believe that only hallucinatory experience is at the base of the tremendous impact this idea has had on civilization. Could a hallucination be the common denominator of all religious thought? Modern phenomena, such as those reported in the Landau case on page 45 can hardly be accounted for by dream theory.

There is a universal unconscious (often conscious) desire to fly. Dreams and fantasies of flight are a common outgrowth of this desire. But, let us consider the possibility of that desire's manifesting itself as a real, objective experience. One way that it has done so is the invention of airplanes to carry our bodies through the skies, or spacecraft that propel people even farther away from the planet. Sky diving, pole vaulting, ski jumping, and hang gliding seem to be some recreational expressions of this desire.

But suppose our desire for flight did not ideally necessitate our taking the body along. Leaving the body behind removes objectivity from the experience and in order to validate it for ourselves, we rely on subjective impressions. Can we trust our opinions and perceptions of our most unusual experiences or is it easier to cast them aside with words like imaginary or uncanny or inexplicable? In the case of spontaneous OBES, especially in near-death experiences where patients are resuscitated or in high falls or other accidents, experients refuse to be convinced by rationalizations that they were merely hallucinating. But more important, their view of life or concept of reality is usually radically altered by the experience. A fantasy of flight may require a body in motion, but true flight may have no need for such a vehicle.

Indians, Europeans, Eskimos, Americans, Moslems, Africans, Hebrews, Chinese, from aborigines to Friends of the Royal Society — the stories and beliefs in mind-body separation emerge again and again. For instance, the North American Huron, Seneca, and other Iroquoian peoples in the seventeenth century ascribed to the soul several faculties, including its capacity to leave the body during dreams or after death. Anthropologist Anthony Wallace, who made a study of these Indians, states: "Intuitively, the Iroquois had achieved a great degree of psychological sophistication."

In 1978, a cross-cultural study by Shiels revealed that only three of 44 societies did *not* hold a belief in OBES (see page 57). The descriptors, means of travel, and purposes for which one projects oneself vary, but the experiential pattern that emerges across cultures is analogous to a patchwork quilt created by many women but ending up a total piece of art of perfect harmony and considerable symmetry.

Erika Bourguignon did a similar cross-cultural survey on trance and spirit possession. She was able to obtain data from 488 world societies — a sample constituting about 57 percent of all societies. She found

> some institutionalized form of dissociation in 437 societies, or 89 percent of the total [sample].... Of these 38 percent (186) had Trance, 27 percent (135) had Possession Trance and 24 percent (116) had both. Furthermore, there were marked differences in worldwide distribution. Thus, 71 percent of all North American Indian societies had Trance, 21 percent had both and a mere 4 percent had only Possession Trance. In contrast to this, in Sub-Saharan Africa, we found only 16 percent of our sample societies to have Trance and 20 percent both forms of institutionalized altered states of consciousness.
>
> These figures are cited here to indicate that we are dealing, indeed, with phenomena of major ethnographic and theoretical significance.[6]

Bourguignon tells us that trance societies are simplistic and that possession trance societies are most complex — that is, have the largest population and the largest local group, stratification, slavery, sedentary settlement pattern, and a complex hierarchy of jurisdictional levels. It would appear that the more complex the society, the more rules are needed to keep everyone in order, the more one needs to escape that kind of rigidity. In overcrowded conditions in India and Japan for instance, it is not uncommon to see people meditating in public, mentally but not bodily removed from the hectic scene around them.

Greek mythology, medieval legends, ancient folklore, nineteenth-century literature, and contemporary science fiction are a few of the categories of writing that describe OBES. Guy de Maupassant, Fyodor Dostoevsky, George du Maurier, Jack London, Thomas Hardy, just to mention a few authors, dealt with the idea of the double in their lives and in their works. Otto Rank discusses many of these ideas in *The Double*. He comments on folklore, mythology, and philological considerations, demonstrating that the double has its origin in one's shadow and reflection. He believes this is where people first derived their conception of an immortal soul.

Understanding OBES, no matter how difficult the task, will undoubtedly coordinate and explain a lot about psychic phenomena, as well as life itself. Maybe all of life's experiences are hallucinatory for prisoners in bodies, as is suggested by Plato's cave allegory. Maybe a true understanding of hallucinations is what is basically needed at this time. Controversy is required for breakthroughs in these areas. Interdisciplinary studies must be coordinated. William James put it nicely, "In psychology, physiology, and medicine, wherever a debate between the mystics and the scientifics has been once for all decided, it is the mystics who have usually proved to be right about the *facts*, while the scientifics had the better of it in respect to the theories."[7]

End Notes

[1]W.Y. Evans-Wentz, *The Tibetan Book of the Dead* (London: Oxford University Press, 1936), p. 92.

[2]*Ibid.*, pp. 31-32.

[3]D. Scott Rogo, "Astral Projection in Tibetan Buddhist Literature," *International Journal of Parapsychology* 10 (1968):277-284. Discusses OBES cited in ancient Tibetan writings.

[4]G.R.S. Mead, *The Doctrine of the Subtle Body in Western Tradition* (London: Stuart & Watkins, 1919). Small paperback outlining most characteristic features of the subtle body as held by Western classical antiquity.

[5]David Starr Jordan, "The Posthom Phantom: A Study in the Spontaneous Activity of Shadows," *Science* 9 (May 12, 1899):674-681. A book review of Adolph D'Assier's *Posthumous Humanity: A Study of Phantoms*.

[6]Erika Bourguignon, "Dreams and Altered States of Consciousness in Anthropological Research," in *Psychological Anthropology*, ed. F.L.K. Hsu (Cambridge, Mass.: Schenkman, 1972), p. 418.

[7]William James, *The Will to Believe* (reprinted New York: Dover, 1956), p. 302.

Chapter V
Evidence from the Lab

Although the out-of-body experience might be considered to be what Jung termed an archetypal experience (an experience potentially available to many members of the human race because it is a basic psychological experience of humans), case studies suggest that the experience may be objective, as well as subjective.[1]

Recent surveys indicate that many people have had at least one OBE in their lives. Celia Green[2] asked two samples of undergraduates from two British universities whether they had ever had an "experience in which you felt you were 'out of your body'?" Of the 115 people in the first sample, 19 percent answered "yes"; and of the 380 people in the second sample even more, 34 percent, said they had. Hornell Hart[3] reported that 27 percent of 155 Duke University sociology students claimed to have had an OBE; and Charles Tart[4] reported that 44 percent of 150 experienced marijuana users gave positive responses. In this mixed sample of 800 cases, then, 32 percent of the people who were asked said that they had had an OBE. For comparison, 32 percent of the United States population would be about 75 million people.

Society at large has been fairly ignorant of these experiences, and so it would seem suggestion alone cannot be influencing the many people to whom they occur spontaneously. Nor could suggestion easily explain OBES in very young children who could not have obtained objective information about them. People ignorant of OBE phenomenon often label reports like these from children, "childhood fantasy." However, accounts of the experiences from independent sources show resemblances to one another. The experience usually has a profound effect on the ex-

41

perient that is long-lasting and may radically change his or her relation to life and death. For instance, Robert Crookall analyzed over 700 nonveridical reports (reports that could not be verified) of OBES and found that 81 percent of these experients had a firm conviction of life after death owing to their personal OBE.[5] The experient will usually hold the conviction that the experience was real in the face of disbelief from everyone around and will often not talk about it to those who may invalidate it, because of its personal value. Skeptics, who believe OBES are mere wish-fulfillment, might have an OBE merely by wishing it.

Pioneer psychic researchers in the nineteenth century debated whether there could be an objective OBE. A case that caused great debate was that of a Mrs. Wilmot:

> Mr. S.R. Wilmot sailed from Liverpool to New York, passing through a severe storm. During the eighth night of the storm he had a dream in which he saw his wife come to the door of the stateroom. She looked about and seeing that her husband was not the only occupant of the room, hesitated a little, then advanced to his side, stooped down and kissed him, and after gently caressing him for a few moments, quietly withdrew.
>
> Upon awakening from this dream, Mr. Wilmot was surprised to hear his fellow passenger, Mr. William J. Tait, say to him: "You're a pretty fellow to have a lady come and visit you in this way."
>
> Pressed for an explanation, Mr. Tait related what he had seen while wide awake, lying in his berth. It exactly corresponded with the dream of Mr. Wilmot!
>
> When meeting his wife in Watertown, Conn., Mr. Wilmot was almost immediately asked by her: "Did you receive a visit from me a week ago Tuesday?"
>
> Although Mr. Wilmot had been more than a thousand miles at sea on that particular night, his wife asserted: "*It seemed to me that I visited you.*" She told her husband that on account of the severity of the weather and the reported loss of another vessel, she had been extremely anxious about him. On the night of the occurrence she had lain awake for a long time and at about four o'clock in the morning it seemed to her that she left her physical self and went out to seek her husband, crossing the stormy sea until she came to his stateroom.
>
> She continued: "A man was in the upper berth, *looking right at me*, and for a moment I was afraid to go in; but soon I went up to the side of your berth, bent down and kissed you, and embraced you, and then went away."[6]

Eleanor Sidgwick, who originally reported this case, accorded it to "travelling clairvoyance," that is, a correct ESP impression of a distant scene coupled with a fantasy of being there. She felt Mr. Wilmot may have had a hallucination of his wife's presence and Mr. Tait may have been telepathically sympathetic to it to a point of seeing it himself.[7] F.W.H. Myers formulated a theory of a "phantasmogenetic centre," which could occupy or modify a part of space.[8] In the Wilmot case, he felt that Mrs. Wilmot discerned material objects from a point of view outside her own organism. He said that "Mr. Tait's seeing a figure at the same time as Mr. Wilmot ... tends to show that Mrs. Wilmot was actually there in some sense other than a purely mental one."

Frank Podmore and Edmund Gurney, also English psychic researchers, tended to think of these experiences as complex telepathic hallucinations, similar to Sidgwick's idea. If collective sightings of apparitions were telepathic, however, it would seem that one would see the apparition from the point of view of the telepathic sender. In fact, people have reported seeing an apparition from the point of view where they were standing in relation to the other percipients. Other factors which contradict the telepathic or hallucinatory theory include reports that doubles have been projected to designated locations and have been seen there by others and that there is usually a purpose involved in projections.

The French physiologist Richet rejected OBES initially, but after many years of psychic research, decided they were "probably not mere hallucinations." G.N.M. Tyrrell, who studied apparitions extensively, said "no" to Myers' theory. On the other hand, Crookall and Hart were so convinced of the experience, they felt it provided basic evidence for the survival of human personality beyond bodily death.

French researchers were the first to work with human subjects on this problem. In their laboratories, they tried to have the exteriorized body move material objects, produce raps at a distance, and affect photographic plates and calcium sulphide screens. They also tried to photograph the exteriorization. Dutch scientists weighed the physical body before, during, and after exteriorization to find a weight loss of 2¼ ounces during exteriorization.[9] McDougall[10] experimented with dying patients and reported weight losses between ⅛ and 1½ ounces at death, but one cannot be sure how carefully controlled the experiments were, or how accurate the equipment was in these early attempts. Alvarado[11] has an interesting article on some of them.

Crookall has done the most thorough compilation and categorizing of spontaneous case reports.[12] From dissections and acute analyses of the anecdotes, he has arrived at a theory as to how OBES operate.[13] He has determined that spontaneous cases usually involve some sort of blackout during separation and reentry. Often the physical body is seen by the double. The experient may be aware of being in an apparitional body that is immune to gravity, and this apparition may be seen by others. Sometimes a panoramic view of past life is seen by the experient; this occurs especially in cases involving falling, drowning, or critical illness. The cases show that various modes of extended consciousness are often experienced, such as telepathy, clairvoyance, precognition, and communication with the deceased. When one enters into these realms of extended consciousness, he or she is often reluctant to return to the body.

Crookall considers natural projection (spontaneous) to be a superior experience to forced projection (through drugs, forcing techniques, falling, and so forth). He reports that consciousness seems clearer in the natural projection and conditions are more peaceful and less confused.

From his analyses of more than 700 cases, Crookall concludes that separation and reentry of the out-of-body entity usually occur in two stages. The first stage may be in the form of a composite double consisting of the "soul body" and a portion of the semiphysical "vehicle of vitality." While the "vehicle of vitality" enshrouds the soul body, the percipient may experience a gloom-enshrouded, Hades-like environment. In the second stage, the double sheds the "vehicle of vitality" and becomes simple—soul body only. Optimum conditions are then experienced, that is, one can see clearly, move freely, and if one is in an otherworldly environment, it appears bright, beautiful, and heavenlike.

As to this hypothesis of two-stage exit and reentry, Crookall states, "In the entire history of psychology no one has described either mental images or 'archetypes' that appear, and disappear, in two stages!"[14] He disagrees with many psychiatrists who consider OBES to be mere mental images by stating, "these seem to be the only 'mental images' which (a) move to a desired place or person and (b) are, on some occasions, actually seen there by other persons."[15]

Celia Green at Oxford University did a psychological

study of over 300 cases of OBE.[16] She points out characteristics of the experience but usually no statistical test was carried out to check for validity of statements. She feels some form of stress, for example, illness or accident, generally precedes a spontaneous OBE. Eighty percent of her sample had what she calls an asomatic experience, that is, they felt themselves to be a disembodied consciousness or point of view in space. Most of Crookall's subjects had reported what Green considers parasomatic experiences, that is, they felt themselves in another body connected via a cord to the physical body.

In Green's sample, the greatest proportion of cases occurred when the person was lying down or in a position of least muscle tone. Muscular tension would seem to keep one's attention on the body, whereas relaxation should increase the possibility for dissociation. There do seem to be basic differences in projecting as a result of stress or relaxation. In a crisis-situation OBE, one is often delighted to have escaped from the physical or psychic pain and may enjoy an asomatic experience with little desire to return to the body. A parasomatic experience may emerge out of a relaxed state, but fear may drive the entity back into its familiar surrounding, that is, into the body.

Hearing is the sensory modality reported second most often in OBES after sight, which occurs 93 percent of the time, according to Green. The other sensory modalities that occur, in order of frequency, are touch, temperature, smell, and taste. Perception and intellectual faculties are reported to be unimpaired in OBES. However, one usually feels like a passive observer rather than an analytic thinker during an OBE.

Sensations of naturalness, completeness, reality, lightness, freedom, vitality, health, elation, and superiority are reported. A person will often react to an OBE with surprise or fear or both. The fear usually results from lack of control of movements and the idea that one will not be able to get back into the body, in other words, fear of death.

Sometimes a person will not only be able to see from another location in space but will actually be able to create an effect at a distance, if we can believe the numerous claims. The Landau case is one of the best examples of this.[17] A Mr. Landau reports that in 1955 his wife-to-be often told him about her OBES. One night he gave her his diary weighing 38 grams and asked her to transport it to his room in her next OBE. Early dawn the next day he awoke and followed her apparition, which backed out of his room across a landing to her room. There he saw her body asleep in bed and then watched the apparition vanish. When he returned to his room he found her rubber toy dog, which weighed 107.5 grams, lying beside his bed. He had last seen it on a chest of drawers in her room. She said the dog was easier for her to transport despite its additional weight, because she had been taught, as a child, never to handle other people's letters or diaries. Moral considerations would therefore still seem to be operative during an OBE and would influence behavior (this is similar to what happens in hypnosis).

Around 1952, sociologist Hornell Hart made a study of spontaneous and experimental cases of what he called ESP projection.[3] Just as the occultists have different names for the OBE, scientists coin their own terms for it also. Hart described three types of experimental cases: (1) projections induced by means of hypnosis, (2) projections by means of concentration, and (3) projections using specific techniques such as those developed by Oliver Fox and Sylvan Muldoon. He listed characteristics of the veridical cases (those giving facts about the real world that were later verified), and they were quite similar to those Crookall found in analyzing hundreds of anecdotal OBES. This indicates that both types of experience may be equally suitable for analysis, since they seem to be of the same intrinsic nature. He found that hypnotically projected individuals reported detailed observations of people and of physical objects and events encountered during their excursions, whereas individuals who self-projected by concentration were more often observed as apparitions, but lacked awareness of being present at the place where their apparitions were seen.

Hart reasoned that projection could provide the basis for a repeatable experiment, and he felt the best experimentation could be done with a sufficient series of hypnotic sessions. Sporadic attempts have been made to test this idea, but none have been successfully completed and reported in the scientific literature. He also thought an objective projection of viewpoint could be confirmed, in fully developed cases, by perceptual organization and positioning of material to be perceived and by having the projectionist report in detail what was seen and where it was seen from. This idea has been carried out in later research but not yet to the point where it would positively rule out all other ESP hypotheses, such as telepathy, clairvoyance, and precognition. It could well be that ESP is a component of an OBE rather than an independent experience.

Hart found no significant causal association between projection and mental pathology. He did feel that being in a state of emotional tension or frustration relative to some person absent at a distance could act as an impetus for an OBE, that is to say, a strong enough desire or need to be with someone could trigger a projection to that person.

Charles Tart was the first person to do psychophysiological studies of people who reported having an OBE. He worked with Robert Monroe in a sleep laboratory at the University of Virginia.[18] The evidence for OBE was inconclusive. Monroe chiefly exhibited stage-1 and stage-2 sleep patterns on his EEG with an absence of rapid eye movements.

Tart's next subject was a woman who showed very slow alpha (alphoid) brain-wave activity when she was reportedly out of her body; the term alpha refers to brain-wave activity in the 8 to 13 cycles per second range, which typically appears in EEGs when one is relaxed with eyes closed.[19] (Monroe has also shown some alphoid activity.) The amplitude (height) of her brain waves also seemed to decrease at the times of projection. There was a decrease in REMs. Heart rate, respiration, circulation, and skin conductivity were all normal. Since REMs typically indicate that a sleeper is dreaming, the absence of or a decrease in REMs during OBEs suggests that whatever OBEs are, they are not dreams.

This study was conducted in a sleep laboratory and on the fourth night, the woman correctly reported a five-digit number that was on a card lying on a high shelf well out of her visual range. Her body movements were controlled and measured by the physiological equipment so she could not have physically gotten up to the shelf to view the target number. It would not have been necessary for her to obtain another viewpoint in space (that is, go out of her body) to ascertain the target since telepathy, clairvoyance, or precognition could have been the means of obtaining the information. In addition, there was a weak possibility that the target constituted a subliminal stimulus in its reflection from a plastic clock surface in the experimental room.

Similar experiments were conducted at the American Society for Psychical Research and produced highly significant results with Ingo Swann (see Chapter I), but conclusive evidence for the OBE are still difficult to establish. For physiological comparison with other cases reported in this chapter, Swann's EEG showed a low-voltage mixed pattern when he reported being exterior. In other words, the EEG showed a mixture of slow, medium, and fast brain waves of low amplitude, sometimes superimposed on one another. This is comparable to alpha blocking—suppression of alpha waves; typical in one who is paying close attention to something. The decrease in the amplitude of the EEG during OBES was more marked in the right brain hemisphere than the left. A decrease in REMs was noted, but his heart rate and other functions of the autonomic nervous system remained normal.[20]

The type of response errors that Swann made with concrete targets suggested right-hemisphere processing. For instance, he was successful with color and shape of target but generally could not name the object. However, spatial difficulties such as right/left or up/down reversals were frequent as he learned to see the multiple-aspect target in the optical image device.

I believe Karlis Osis at the ASPR has developed the best experimental method to date for separating an objective OBE from ESP coupled with the sensation of traveling or being at a distant point in space. His design simultaneously tests (1) perception (whether the OBE subject can perceive a distant target constructed so that it can be seen only from a particular point in space); (2) physical changes in the target-viewing area (for example, changes in electrostatic fields or kinetic effects); and (3) physiological changes (for example, in the brain waves) in the person who is attempting to have an OBE. The participant is isolated from the target in a soundproof room about 60 feet from the target, with five walls intervening. No one knows what the exact target is. The complex optical image device, which automatically randomizes and presents the target, rules out telepathy and makes clairvoyance extremely difficult.

If the participant correctly identifies the target, and at the same time definite and recurring EEG patterns accompany the perception, and at the same time a detector also registers some sort of change in the physical space in the viewing area, one may be led to believe an objective OBE has occurred. In other words, if a person reports being there in front of the optical image device, sees the target normally, exhibits specific brain-wave patterns, and a presence is registered by the detectors in that location, then one could fairly say that in some sense she or he *is* there.

Osis and Boneita Perskari,[21] with the help of others, spent several years designing and developing the equipment and procedures for this experiment and screening and testing individuals. There were certain difficulties inherent in the task. For instance, if there is some quasiphysical out-of-body entity that can interact with the physical world, what kind of detector would register it? Since nothing is known of its nature, one can only guess at what kind of detector would be suitable. The obvious and readily available detection systems such as various kinds of photographic film, videotape, and a Geiger counter were employed without success while other more subtle types of detectors were being designed and built.

But even more importantly, although many people have had a spontaneous OBE, it is extremely difficult to find those who can produce OBES at will during a laboratory session. Of the very few who can produce a subjective OBE, there are even fewer who can paranormally gain information about the target, and most of these give only the partially correct responses that could be attributed to telepathy or clairvoyance rather than the wholly correct responses indicative of OBE-type vision. Probably not one in a hundred of those persons who can produce a subjective OBE at will are capable of producing ten trials (guesses at the target) in a laboratory session that even begin to suggest OBE vision rather than general ESP.

Perskari worked closely with Alex Tanous for several years at the ASPR. She believes that his test results suggest that with practice he might be able to consistently give OBE-type results on the perceptual, or target-viewing part of the experiment. If individuals could train themselves to do this consistently, it might then be only a matter of time until the proper detector is found. The perceptual-test results alone, although very suggestive, are not enough to demonstrate an objective OBE; they must be coupled with evidence from some sort of physical (not human or animal) detector.

Osis and Donna McCormick[22] reported on further experiments with Tanous. In this data, the optical image device was coupled with a sensor in the viewing location which could detect unintentional mechanical effects. Strain-gauge sensors in a shielded chamber in front of the viewing window of the optical image device were more active when Tanous gave correct responses to perceptual targets than on trials where he could not identify them. The results were seen to conform with the separationist theory of OBES, that is, that some part of his consciousness seemed to be separate from his body.

Tanous is continuing his efforts to give clear, consistent, repeatable results on these tests. If an objective OBE exists, I feel this experimental approach is the only one so far proposed that might be able to definitely verify it.

The big advantage at the ASPR is that participants are always conscious, whereas Tart had worked with people who seemed to find it necessary to go to sleep in order to leave their bodies. There seems to be a conscious evolution of the experience over the last hundred years: more people today than in the past seem to be able to get the experience under conscious control and share information as to how they are able to do it, and the "silver cord" that purportedly attached the double to the body is no longer reported with such frequency—almost as if it were the umbilical cord that has now been severed to release the modern experients into an independent and less fearful stage of being.

John Palmer's attempts to investigate OBES produced no conclusive evidence for the experience.[23] Robert Morris and others,[24] on the other hand, tried animal detectors as indicators of an out-of-body presence. Two kittens were placed into a three-foot-deep "open field" container with a 30 by 80 inch floor divided into 24 numbered squares 10 inches on a side. The kittens' owner, Blue Harary, was in another building about one-half mile away, trying to project during designated periods and make his presence known to the kittens. Kitten behavioral measures were meows per 100 seconds and squares entered per 100 seconds. Entering a square meant placing both forepaws into it.

There was one striking result in four experimental sessions with the kitten that showed most promise in the pilot study. The kitten meowed 37 times during eight control periods, but not once during eight OBE experimental periods. Odds against the vocalizations occurring by chance were 200 to 1 and odds against the number of squares crossed, 100 to 1.

Data collected from using human detectors in the OBE projection area were less convincing, and physical (mechanical/ electrical) detectors provided no clues. Physiological data showed a complex picture. There was a significant decrease in skin potential during OBE, which indicated relaxation. At the same time, there was a significant increase in heart rate and respiration, indicating arousal. There was a decrease in REMS as seen in other studies, and it was determined that Harary's EEG records during OBES did not resemble his regular EEG sleep and dream patterns.

One other bit of physiological data has come from Joel Whitton in Canada where he reports a "ramp function" when Alex Tanous reported being out of his body.[25] Using a sophisticated computer to analyze the EEG data, Whitton could obtain power-spectrum estimates showing the relative amounts of energy produced by the brain at different frequencies, and his "ramp function" is described as one in which most of the energy is in the lower EEG frequencies (peaks occurring in the 1 to 4 cycles per second range). In appearance, it is a flattening of the EEG record as reported by Tart and Osis and Mitchell.

This is a very difficult area for research, but the ASPR seems to be leading the way to verifying this experience. The implications of a finding that OBES are objective events would have tremendous impact on the currently held societal self-image. The near-death cases reported by Noyes and Slymen[26] and Raymond Moody[27] are already stimulating society at large to move toward a rethinking of its concepts about survival of bodily death. Laboratory confirmation of objective OBES would strengthen positive beliefs in personal survival.

End Notes

[1]Robert J. Crookall, *The Jung-Jaffé View of Out-of-the-Body Experiences* (London: World Fellowship Press, 1970). Jung and Jaffé consider OBES to be archetypal experiences originating in the collective unconscious and Crookall argues the objectivity of the etheric or soul body.

[2]Celia Green, "Ecsomatic Experiences and Related Phenomena," *Journal of the Society for Psychical Research* 44 (1967):111-130. Analysis of questionnaires answered by Oxford undergraduates.

[3]Hornell Hart, "ESP Projection: Spontaneous Cases and the Experimental Method," *Journal of the American Society for Psychical Research* 48 (1954):121-146. Analyzes questionnaires and what he considers veridical cases, such as where the experient was seen by others at a distance. Hart advocates hypnosis for experimental use.

[4]Charles Tart, *On Being Stoned* (Palo Alto, Calif.: Science and Behavior Books, 1971).

[5]Robert J. Crookall, *Intimations of Immortality* (London: James Clarke, 1965). Discusses the effect of OBES on personal belief in survival of bodily death.

[6]Sylvan Muldoon, *The Case for Astral Projection* (Chicago: Aries Press, 1936), pp. 115-116.

[7]Eleanor Sidgwick, "On the Evidence for Clairvoyance," *Proceedings of the Society for Psychical Research* 7 (1891-1892):41-47.

[8]F.W.H. Myers, "Note on a Suggested Mode of Psychical Interaction," in *Phantasms of the Living*, Vol. 2, ed. by Edmund Gurney, F.W.H. Myers, and Frank Podmore (London: Society for Psychical Research, 1886).

[9]H. Carrington, *Laboratory Investigations into Psychic Phenomena* (Philadelphia: McKay, n.d.).

[10]D. McDougall, "Hypothesis Concerning Soul Substance Together with Experimental Evidence of the Existence of Such Substance," *Journal of the American Society for Psychical Research* 1 (1907):237-244.

[11]C.S. Alvarado, "The Physical Detection of the Astral Body: An Historical Perspective," *Theta* 8 (1980):4-7.

[12]Robert J. Crookall, *The Study and Practice of Astral Projection* (New Hyde Park, N.U.: University Books, 1966); *More Astral Projections* (Hackensack, N.J.: Wehman, 1964); *Casebook of Astral Projection*, 545-746 (New Hyde Park, N.Y.: University Books, 1972). These three books contain over 500 cases of astral projections with commentary and theory.

[13]Robert J. Crookall, *Out-of-the-Body Experiences* (New Hyde Park, N.Y.: University Books, 1970); *The Next World—and the Next* (London: Theosophical Publishing House, 1966). Discussion of Crookall's theories about how the double is released and returned to the body and of the often-debated issue of clothing seen in doubles.

[14]Crookall, *Out-of-the-Body Experiences*, p. 134.

[15]*Ibid.*, p. 124.

[16]Celia Green, *Out-of-the-Body Experiences* (New York: Ballantine, 1973).

[17]Lucian Landau, "An Unusual Out-of-the-Body Experience," *Journal of the Society for Psychical Research* 42 (1963):126-128. Detailed report of a woman transporting a toy dog from one room to another during an OBE and being seen as an apparition.

[18]Charles Tart, "A Second Psychophysiological Study of Out-of-the-Body Experiences in a Gifted Subject," *International Journal of Parapsychology* 9 (1967):251-258. First scientific report of EEG concomitants to OBES.

[19]Charles Tart, "A Psychophysiological Study of Out-of-the-Body Experiences in a Selected Subject," *Journal of the American Society for Psychical Research* 62 (1968):3-27.

[20]K. Osis and J.L. Mitchell, "Physiological Correlates of Re-

ported Out-of-Body Experiences," *Journal of the Society for Psychical Research* **49** (1977):525-536.

²¹K. Osis and B. Perskari, "Perceptual Tests of the Out-of-Body Hypothesis," report distributed by the Chester F. Carlson Research Laboratory, American Society for Psychical Research, 1975.

²²K. Osis and D. McCormick, "Kinetic Effects at the Ostensible Location of an Out-of-Body Projection during Perceptual Testing," *Journal of the American Society for Psychical Research* **74** (1980):319-329.

²³J. Palmer and C. Vassar, "ESP and Out-of-the-Body Experiences: An Exploratory Study," *Journal of the American Society for Psychical Research* **68** (1974):257-280; and J. Palmer and R. Lieberman, "The Influence of Psychological Set on ESP and Out-of-Body Experiences," *Journal of the American Society for Psychical Research* **69** (1975):193-213.

²⁴R.L. Morris, S.B. Harary, J. Janis, J. Hartwell, and W.G. Roll, "Studies of Communication during Out-of-Body Experiences," *Journal of the American Society for Psychical Research* **72** (1978):1-21.

²⁵J.L. Whitton, "'Ramp Functions' in EEG Power Spectra during Actual or Attempted Paranormal Events," *New Horizons* **1** (1974):174-183.

²⁶Russell Noyes, Jr., and D.J. Slymen, "The Subjective Response to Life-Threatening Danger," *Omega* **9** (4) (1978-79):313-321.

²⁷Raymond Moody, *Life After Life* (New York: Bantam/ Mockingbird, 1975).

Chapter VI

Is an OBE a Dream or Are Dreams Just OBEs?

The purpose of this chapter is to provide you with knowledge gained by others through studies concerning dreams and out-of-body experiences or through personal experiences deemed important enough to record. But more importantly, it is to guide you in your own experiential awareness.

The latest scientific finding on dreams and OBES comes from Osis at the American Society for Psychical Research. In the spring of 1978, he, Donna McCormick, and I did a computerized frequency analysis of 304 OBE questionnaires he had accumulated. Each experient responded to 96 items. In the July 1978 *ASPR Newsletter*, Osis reported that "the vast majority contend that OBE vision is different from both ESP and dream imagery." Only 4 percent found dream imagery to be similar to OBE vision. This suggests that although dreams and OBES may share some characteristics, there is a distinguishable difference for the experient.

Stuart "Blue" Harary, in a personal communication (1972), differentiated precognitive dreams from OBES initiated during sleep:

> OBES to future time and space differ from regular precognitive dreams in that I am definitely "out" and moving through a black, dark area that ends at some lighted future scene. The scene is seen by looking through a "window" that is like a silhouette of myself as I will be in the scene. Upon returning, I awaken and can remember only vaguely that I have been out and cannot remember much about where I have been. When the future scene becomes the present time and space, I get a sensation of nearly blacking out (nearly!) and then I re-

54

member the OBE vividly. There is a very strong feeling of déjà vu and then a sensation that I can only describe as meeting myself "behind" myself as if I were two beings. I feel as if the me of the present were encountering the OBE of the past who traveled into the future.... Lately, I've been experiencing normal precognitive dreams more often than OBES. This may be a function of state of mental consciousness. Precognitive dreams are more easily remembered than OBES and are readily identifiable as dreams upon awakening (and to some extent while they are occurring, since I often know when I am dreaming because I can feel my entire self in one place on the bed rather than in several places). When the precognitive dream [later] occurs in reality (whatever that is), déjà vu is also experienced but without the feelings of slipping into another state of consciousness that accompany OBE-déjà vu's. I do not get a feeling anything like "meeting myself behind myself" when living through what was a precognitive dream either. I remain quite conscious and aware of what is going on around me during precognitive déjà vu's.

When I once asked Blue to tell me the difference between realization in an OBE and in a dream, he said it was as clearcut as being in a room and dreaming about being in that room.

Personal experimenters have repeatedly stated that OBES are not glorified dreams. Ingo Swann would probably protest vigorously if one were to give the name "dreams" to his exteriorizations. He is only one of the increasing number of experients who claim to be able to exteriorize from their bodies with perception, decision-making abilities, and memory while in a waking state. Alex Tanous, who is now the prime experient being tested at the ASPR, also claims to leave his body consciously and at will. There have been some results that suggest these claims may have some validity and are worthy of further laboratory study. Blue Harary also does not need to go to sleep in order to have an OBE. Early experimental work by Charles Tart was done in the 1960s in sleep laboratories, but our modern experients seem to have more control over their experiences than their earlier counterparts.

Robert Monroe in his book, *Journeys Out of the Body*, has the following to say about flying and falling dreams. He appears to classify some dreams as OBES with insufficient consciousness and memory:

> I am quite certain that such dreams are but memories of some degree of Second State experience [OBE]. I have often become aware of experiencing the flying dream during sleep, only to

discover that I was actually floating out in the Second Body as I brought consciousness to the incident. This involuntary action happens most frequently without any conscious effort. It may well be that many people do have this experience during sleep, but just don't remember it. A dream of riding or flying in an airplane has a similar connotation.... Falling dreams were also repeatedly examined in my early experiments. It is a common "feeling" in quick reintegration of the Second Body with the physical. Evidently, the proximity of the physical causes it to accept relayed sensory signals from the Second, which is "falling" into the physical [pp. 187-188].

Monroe has always been concerned that the psychological and psychiatric community is creating mentally ill people by not taking the time to explore and understand patients' personal experiences. It is easier to pigeonhole behaviors and give them worn-out labels than to investigate, define, and validate nonphysical experiences and their meaningfulness to the experient.

If a psychiatrist asks you about your dreams, he or she may show a keen sense of interest in what you relate. If you are asked if you have ever had the feeling of being someplace other than in your body, not much interest will be shown in your experience but it may be used to diagnose your "illness." Indeed, this is used as a diagnostic question. In this society, dreams are okay but OBES are not. If your listener is fond of you, but skeptical, your OBES may be classified as "just" dreams. But personal experimenters, such as Monroe, may suggest the opposite—that dreams are "just" OBES with poorly developed consciousness.

Dreams may be launching pads for OBES. This seems especially true with lucid dreams. A lucid dream is one in which you are aware that you are dreaming and can actually exert some control over the dream content. In other words, if you can increase your awareness during dreaming, you may find that you are not dreaming at all but having a totally different type of experience similar to the waking state but without the physical vehicle (body).

Oliver Fox used what he called the *dream of knowledge* as a technique for leaving his body. What he describes is similar to what is now called a lucid dream. He would try to keep his critical faculty awake while he physically went to sleep and then try to discern any discrepancy in a scene so that he might realize he was dreaming.

Objects are often transformed in strange ways in dreams. For instance, you may dream that you are driving down the road in your car, but suddenly find yourself on horseback. You may then realize that the transformation of a car into a horse is impossible and that therefore you must be dreaming. Once you have realized this, you can wake up or you can simply watch the dream unfold or you can try to guide your horse to a specific destination and see what is going on there, and then when you awaken, check to see whether what you saw there actually took place or not. If you can begin to pick up correct information in this way, you may through repeated attempts begin to distinguish between "just dreams" and real information gathered while you sleep; and you may be on the way to voluntary, controlled OBES.

We may all have OBES nightly but never realize it — possibly only the awareness is lacking rather than the experience itself. We are told that we have several dreams every night, but there are many mornings when we remember none. If our memory and awareness are so feeble in the face of an ordinary, accepted human experience, consider how crippled they may be in the face of the fear and nonacceptance accorded to reports of OBES.

Dean Shiels reported on an ethnological study concerning beliefs in OBES in 67 non-Western cultures.[1] His idea was to test a dream theory proposed by Sir E.B. Tylor in 1929 which suggested that the rise of belief in the soul and OBE were based on dreaming.[2] For instance, if a sleeper saw and spoke with a dead person during sleep, on awakening he or she might suppose that an immortal soul had survived physical death. To advance to a belief in OBES from this idea is logical: If there is a soul and one experiences being in another place in a dream, one could easily believe the soul had left the body. Shiels tested this theory by determining from his data what proportion of dreams were interpreted as OBES in the different cultures.

He had adequate data on only 44 cultures to perform this type of analysis. In 14 of these societies most (and usually all) dreams were seen as OBES. In a third of the societies, dreams were not interpreted as OBES even though OBE beliefs were present. In some of these cultures it was felt that only shamans could experience OBES. In three of these societies OBE beliefs were absent, so dreams could not be interpreted as OBES. Of the sample, 31 percent distinguished between dreams that are OBES and dreams that are "just" dreams and nothing more. If all members of each population dream but only some special members or no members at all have OBES, then dreams cannot be interpreted as OBES. Tylor's dream theory therefore appears to be inadequate to explain OBE beliefs in a fairly good sample of non-Western cultures.

How often in dreams do we find ourselves in other places with other people, sometimes those who are deceased? But when we awaken, we think that it was only a dream. On the other hand, those who realize OBES awaken and feel that somehow they were actually in a distant place. So in the unconscious state, there appears to be two different experiences just as we can have two experiences in the waking state: thinking of being in another place and actually going there. The sensations of physically going to another place can never be mistaken for fantasizing being there, but in the unconscious state it is possible that going somewhere in a mental body (which is taboo) may be considered only a dream.

Defense mechanisms may be put into operation to keep our experience from conscious realization because with every new freedom there is added responsibility. Can we assume the responsibility for being able to move about and have effects while in invisible form? A need for a different order of ethics is apparent here. The adamant argument which implies that OBES are dreams indicates that we are not yet ready for the increased responsibility.

Nor do we seem to be ready to accept a new self-image that declares our spiritual beingness. We have been too cleverly and consistently taught that we are bodies by materialistic philosophies and behavioristic psychologies. Although physical scientists can withstand uprooting of established theories, unstable social scientists cling to their theories, whether proven or not.

But, there is a far more important personal idea that prevents us from realizing our experiences in the mental body and that is fear of death. Robert Monroe has been trying to train people to leave their bodies for years, and he states that the fear of not being able to return to their bodies is the major stumbling block. In some cultures, people are careful not to awaken a person too rapidly for fear that the soul will not have sufficient time to return and take control of the body. Therefore, they are actually afraid of killing other persons by awakening them too suddenly. Have deaths occurred in this manner? I know of none. But we do know how very unpleasant it is to be jarred from sleep by a loud noise or violent movement.

Contrary to this stated fear of death, Karlis Osis has determined through his research as reported in *At the Hour of Death*[3] that fear is not typically the dominant emotion as one dies. There are reports of near-death experiences where the person wished to leave the body permanently but felt forced by subtle forms or audible commands to return and continue life in the body.

It is so much easier for us to think that some inexplicable experience was a dream than to think it was an OBE. Conformity is comfortable — in present-day society, one is not intellectually rejected for reporting a dream. A dream can be forgotten and it need never trouble our thinking processes again. If we were to accept the reality of an OBE, we would have to withstand the pressure of disagreeing with society's concept of reality for the rest of our days. In practically every spontaneous case of OBE that has been acknowledged, the experient stresses the profound effect of the experience on the rest of his or her life — effects concerning the way in which one views oneself, the world, life, and death. In this anxiety-ridden world, can we accept this additional pressure? Or, is it in fact the only way to our freedom? Can we begin to view the body as our anchor to the physical world, or must we continue to be imprisoned by it?

A good way to start to free ourselves is to begin to feel and know our experiences for what they are, in the face of every contradictory argument. I have described below some techniques for personal investigation. There will always be those to discourage these pursuits. Conformity is important in a densely populated, technological nation, but personal nonconformity that allows one to enjoy his or her own unique experiences and learn from them is also essential. You are the only one who has your exact experience. Take the initiative to realize and begin to understand your own experiences for their own personal value, while maintaining a cautious attitude toward self-delusion. Do not let others limit you, and by all means do not limit yourself in the realm of experience. We are here to live and to live abundantly.

First, you might like to consider a method for analyzing your dreams. Frederik Van Eeden began to study his dreams in 1896. In 1913 his first report, "A Study of Dreams," was published in London.[4] He classified different types of dreams and was particularly interested in lucid dreams. He experienced and recorded more than 350 lucid dreams as a part of his study.

He concluded he had a "dream-body" and that he could "remember as clearly the action of the dream-body as the restfulness of the physical body." He did not classify dreams as OBES, but he did speak about a continuum of dreaming from floating and flying to lucid dreams. He mentions an astral body when speaking of his dream-body and then emphasizes the distinct sensation of having a body in certain dreams. Van Eeden considered this short, easy-to-read article as only a preliminary sketch of a greater work, which apparently he was never able to complete.

How can you differentiate ordinary dreams, lucid dreams, and OBES? Attention to your experience is crucial, but *intention* may be even more meaningful. Therefore, tonight as you go to sleep you may use the powerful forces of suggestion to increase your awareness. To become aware of more than common, chaotic dream content, you may try affirming, "I will be conscious that I am dreaming in my dreams tonight." If you have difficulty remembering your dreams at all, you may start your mental exercises by affirming, "I will remember my dreams tonight." Dream structure will shift to accommodate your own personal assumptions, expectations, and intention. Changing these personal views is the key to working consciously with the dream state. Expectancy cannot be underestimated in influencing our experience, so to expect to have a lucid dream is fine but to expect the actual shape it may take could prove limiting. It is better to expect things such as that it will be pleasant and important for your personal growth.

As a technique, try something personally motivating. For instance, going to bed thirsty may cause you to dream you are in a desert with no water or it may cause you to move out of your body in order to satisfy your thirst, as Sylvan Muldoon suggests.[5]

You may also use intention to obtain freedom and peace on an inner level. Once you have brought lucidity to your dreams, you may try the following experiment. If you are having a nightmare, confront the frightening entity in an effort to learn its purpose. If you get no satisfaction, but continued threats, remove the presence from your dreams. You can visualize doing this with anything from a pencil eraser to a hydrogen bomb. Some will prefer to surround the entity with love and light. You could also just announce in the dream, "You are only a figment of my imagination." If you are in any sort of confining enclosure in the dream, dissolve it. Above all, remember that you are the producer-director of your dreams. By maintaining peace and freedom in your dreams, you may experience a new peacefulness in your waking state, as well. Decreasing inner anxiety will release waking energy and probably help to relieve feelings of depression.

Now that you are enjoying lucid dreams in which you are able to exercise some control over your experience rather than the symbolic, chaotic dreaming that is little understood, suppose you desire to have an OBE. Try saying to yourself something like, "Tonight while I am asleep I am going to consciously leave my body and remember all the details of the experience when I awaken." You may want to travel to a physical location to derive information that can later be verified. Perhaps you will ask a friend to place some object (unknown to you) in full view in a specified room in their home; you can try to identify this target object and thus can verify your experience later with an understanding friend. What may happen is that you find yourself in a nonphysical environment. Do not be alarmed. Learn what you can and continue to try to shape your experience to your personal desire. If your quest is to come to know your spiritual beingness, some external verification of your experience will undoubtedly be necessary.

Gaining awareness and control of your dream experiences is certainly a valid way of changing your self-image and, in turn, your personal experiences. Dreams are not OBEs and OBEs are not dreams, but it is up to each of us to learn for ourselves how to discriminate these two altered states of consciousness. You have the assurance that others have tried and succeeded. You need motivation and courage to discern these realms of experience for yourself. It seems you already have the motivation if you are reading this book, and courage is simply the ability to confront what one can imagine.

End Notes

[1]Dean Shiels, "A Cross-Cultural Study of Beliefs in Out-of-the-Body Experiences," *Journal of the Society for Psychical Research* **49** (1978):697-741.

[2]E.B. Tylor, *Primitive Culture* (London: J. Murray, 1871).

[3]Karlis Osis and E. Haraldsson, *At the Hour of Death* (New York: Avon Books, 1977).

[4]Frederik Van Eeden, "A Study of Dreams," *Proceedings of the Society for Psychical Research* **26** (1913):431-461; also in *Altered States of Consciousness*, ed. Charles Tart (Garden City, N.Y.: Doubleday, 1972), pp. 147-160. Fascinating account of early study of dreams. He classifies his dreams into nine experientially distinct types and reports that lucid dreams usually lead to the conception of a "dream-body."

[5]Sylvan Muldoon and H. Carrington, *The Projection of the Astral Body* (New York: Weiser, n.d.), pp. 227-230.

Chapter VII

Phenomena Similar to OBEs

Psychologist Gardner Murphy in his *Challenge of Psychical Research* expressed the opinion that OBES are not very far from the known terrain of general psychology. Paragraphs on OBES are beginning to appear in some general psychology textbooks. In fact, psychiatrists and clinical psychologists have been talking about these experiences for a number of years but using different terminology, such as:

(1) Depersonalization—state in which people lose the feeling of personal reality or feel their bodies to be unreal. Everything seems dreamlike, and actions of oneself or others are watched with indifferent detachment. There may be delusions, such as that the body is hollow or does not exist.

(2) Dissociation—a behavioral disorder, involving repression, in which certain aspects of personality and memory are compartmentalized and function more or less independently; examples are amnesia and multiple personality (weekday sinner—Sunday saint).

(3) Ego splitting—a dissociative reaction to stress characterized by unnatural calm and feeling as though one is outside of oneself.

(4) Autoscopy—seeing an image of oneself at a distance.

Psychiatrists who would try to help patients understand these experiences and their need for them would promote better mental health than those who label the experiences symptoms of illness and maladjustment. Out-of-body phenomena, regardless of what one calls them, have been reported in normal individuals in altered states of consciousness such as hypnosis, in special situations such as sensory deprivation and near-death experiences, and during migraine and epileptic attacks.

63

Psychiatric dictionaries still do not include out-of-body experiences among their definitions. However, it is not unusual for a psychiatrist during an initial interview to include a question such as, "Have you ever experienced yourself as being someplace other than in your body?" If answered in the affirmative, it is usually considered hallucinatory behavior.

Can an OBE be a hallucination or mental image? Two thorough, qualitative analyses of OBE narratives[1] gathered common characteristics of the experiences. Both studies, done independently, reported these five characteristics, although each reported certain additional characteristics not confirmed by the other study:

(1) People saw their own physical bodies during the experience as if they were looking at their bodies from outside.

(2) They experienced themselves in apparitional bodies.

(3) These phantom bodies were immune to gravity.

(4) People sometimes reported observations of distant places or persons that were correct but could not have been known by normal means.

(5) The apparition was sometimes seen by another person at a distant location.

One classical psychoanalytic interpretation of an OBE is that psychic energy somehow gets misdirected within the body and converted into the experience of being apart from the body. One cognitive approach is that of ego splitting. Ego boundaries usually maintained cognitively are somehow blurred, as well as one's conceptual reality about the nature of the boundaries between self and environment. Some researchers have expressed the idea that a loss of muscular signals to the brain, as one might experience in a shock reaction to an accident, is enough to give the impression of being apart from the body.

Depersonalization phenomena sometime include feelings of being separated from one's body but a strict definition of depersonalization syndrome deviates sharply from OBE reports, especially in that depersonalization is "A nonspecific syndrome in which the patient feels that he has lost his personal identity, that he is different or strange or unreal. Derealization, the feeling that the environment is also strange and unreal, is usually part of the syndrome."[2] When Celia Green analyzed hundreds of OBE reports, one of the main things she found was that a person in an out-of-body state feels more real, not less real or unreal.

Psychiatrists began to pay significant attention to depersonalization after World War I. Many of them were aware "that depersonalization could appear as an isolated symptom in patients without any psychiatric complaints."[3] It was decided and published by the American Psychiatric Association in their manual that "A brief experience of depersonalization is not necessarily a symptom of illness."

Nemiah, in describing depersonalization, states that "An occasional and particularly curious phenomenon is that of 'doubleing'; the patient feels that his point of consciousness 'I-ness' is outside of his body, commonly a few feet overhead, from where he actually observes himself as if he were a totally other person."[4] He adds, "Despite the fact that a number of thoughtful clinical investigators have focused their attention on depersonalization, its etiology remains obscure."[5]

Déjà vu is an established psychological phenomenon where that which is in fact new, alien, and previously unexperienced is felt as being familiar and as having been perceived before, whereas in depersonalization what is actually familiar is sensed as strange, novel, and unreal. If depersonalization is a psychiatric term encompassing OBES, it looks as if déjà vu can be considered a phenomenon in its own right, different from either OBES or depersonalization.

Déjà vu may be a type of unconscious precognitive OBE as suggested by Harary's personal correspondence on page 54, however, the main feature of an OBE is pure detached cognition and déjà vu appears to be an emotional response or arousal without specific cognitive or cortical interpretation.

Medical practitioners and psychoanalysts were once interested in an experience they termed autoscopy. The last journal article to be found on the subject is dated 1960.[6] By strict definition, autoscopy is a seeing of one's double in space. Written reports often contain descriptions of people seeing their bodies from a distance, similar to an OBE.

Sigmund Freud had one autoscopic experience. He deals with the topic of doubling in his paper on "The Uncanny." He felt the body image resided in the ego and could be split and reduplicated. At times this could be a defense in which the ego projects material outward as something foreign to itself. It could be a manifestation of primary narcissism or later in adult life it might appear as a harbinger of death. Splitting of the ego might also constitute a normal aspect of development, that is, creation of the superego by detachment of a part of self-observation and ego ideal.

Other authors have made an attempt at etiology of autoscopy, considered hallucinatory behavior. Migraine and epileptic attacks have been suggested as possible causes.[7] Todd and Dewhurst[8] came to the conclusion that "narcissism should be regarded as a *specific* factor facilitating the appearance of visual hallucinations *of the self.*" In visualizers with a narcissistic preoccupation, any organically precipitated visual hallucination might tend to take the shape of an autoscopic double.

Narcissism may take the form of an undue interest in the appearance of one's body, one's physical health, or in the workings of one's mind. Therefore, the authors studied reported autoscopic experiences in narcissistic poets and writers, introspectionists who are preoccupied with their own egos, and cases of hypochrondriacs. They felt that when narcissism was associated in the same person with supernormal powers of visualization, that may predispose him or her to autoscopic experience. In *The Double*, Otto Rank found that authors who made recurrent use of the double motif in their works were characterized by extreme narcissism. He also saw it as an attempt at immortality.

The experiences were also seen as a wish-fulfilling mechanism in some cases, desires for omnipotence, or as an outlet for aggression and sadistic impulses. Other general or predisposing factors that Todd and Dewhurst discovered include chronic alcoholism, anxiety, fatigue, exhaustion, attacks of acute labyrinthe vertigo, and febrile-toxic states of typhus and influenza. Recurrent autoscopia is seen in dementia paralytica, encephalitis lethargica, drug addiction, and schizophrenia. Psychological traits that may be found common in experients are egocentricity, narcissism, and vivid visual imagery.

There is evidence that autoscopic experiences may be brought on by irritation of the cortex as in epilepsy and migraine. Physiological observations are important validation criteria for any altered state of consciousness. Lyle[9] and Bollea[10] have attempted to derive neurological theories as to etiology of autoscopy. The principle organic theory at this point is that irritative lesions in the temporo-parieto-occipital areas may bring on autoscopic hallucinations. Bollea has electrically stimulated posterior zones of the parietal lobes and produced autoscopic visions. Todd and Dewhurst state that this irritative lesion must therefore be accounted among *specific* causes.

Various physiological theories have also been put forward for depersonalization phenomena and Penfield and Rasmussen have demonstrated the association of these phenomena with electrical stimulation to the cortex of the temporal lobes.

Autoscopy has been noted in some focal lesions of the brain, in posttraumatic cerebral lesions, in organic cerebral disease, and cortical atrophy. Although this happens — it is not the rule. Cairns, as cited in Dewhurst,[11] reviewed 800 cases of persons suffering intracranial tumors, of which 100 experienced visual hallucinations but *none* of them saw themselves.

In 1975, a summary article by Lehmann stated that autoscopic phenomena "are as a rule, not symptomatic of any particular mental disorder.... [T]here is possibly a certain relation to migraine and epilepsy.... One theory holds that the phenomenon reflects an irritation of areas in the temporoparietal lobes."[12]

Another instance where one sometimes experiences being apart from the body is a life-threatening situation. In 1980, R.K. Siegel[13] stressed the idea that OBE reports in near-death experiences are common hallucinations. Calling such experiences hallucinations or delusions may solve the problem for Siegel, but if a hallucination is a "sensory experience without known physical basis" and if a delusion is "a belief held in the face of evidence *normally* sufficient to destroy the belief," naming experiences in this manner does not seem to lead one any nearer the truth of the experience. His data and conclusions seem sparse.

Noyes and Slymen[14] did a factor analysis of questionnaire responses from 189 victims of life-threatening accidents and illness and found three major subjective effects, one of which was depersonalization. A majority (58 per cent) of seriously ill patients answered "yes" to the item "body apart from self." A majority of all types of accident and illness patients answered "yes" to the item "self strange or unreal." Drowning and miscellaneous accident victims responded to four of the depersonalization questionnaire items less frequently than did fall or automobile accident victims.

Cloudy consciousness during stress could account for perceptual distortions, but in the above study hyperalertness was reported most frequently (average frequency, 59 per cent) followed by depersonalization (39 per cent) and mystical consciousness items least frequently (26 per cent). These three types of effect appeared meaningful in terms of the personality's attempt to cope with a perceived threat to life.

Noyes reports that 60 per cent of those who believed themselves about to die claimed that their attitude toward death — and life — changed as a consequence of the experience. Only 39 per cent of those who did not believe they had been close to death reported such a change. This is a statistically significant difference in attitude changes that would happen by chance once in a hundred times. If these experiences are hallucinations, as suggested by Siegel, still they produce a profound effect on one's thinking.

In a questionnaire survey of 304 people who had one or more OBEs, Osis and McCormick[15] asked how their experiences altered their philosophies and day-to-day lives. Fantasies are not known to be life-changing experiences, so if their OBEs were fantasies, there should be little change. Beneficial changes were claimed by 88 per cent of the sample. Besides discovering new meanings of life and death, they reportedly saw things in a more holistic way, became aware of spiritual values and new states of consciousness (73 per cent reported new spiritual and philosophical outlooks). Fear of death was diminished in 23 per cent of respondents and completely dismissed by another 43 per cent of the sample. Almost half of the sample reported improved relationships with others and that their work was affected for the better. Fifty per cent reported being either healthier or much healthier mentally after their OBE. When they were asked, "Would you like to have another OBE?" 95 per cent said "Yes."

In both sensory deprivation (SD) and perceptual deprivation (PD) conditions, as one loses contact with reality, external and internal sensations are confused, there is an increase in imaginative thinking, and a disorientation as to time and space. Experiences of being somewhere other than in the body are often reported in these circumstances. Experiments in SD and PD demonstrate how dependent waking consciousness is on external stimulation in order to define body image and conscious ego.[16]

Undergoing SD severely limits one's sensory experiences, with the result that one often loses the physical frame of reference. This is followed by disturbances of one's body image or loosening of one's ego boundaries, or both. Regressive behavior is also common in SD. People who rely more heavily on external cues for orientation have a less differentiated body image and report more depersonalization experiences in SD than introverted people. However, introverts seem to adapt more poorly to isolation and they report more depersonalization experiences in a short SD experience of 20 to 60 minutes. When aggressive feelings are repressed in an SD experiment, depersonalization experiences are more likely to be reported.

Perceptual deprivation consists of conditions of homogenous visual stimulation and white noise as the only auditory stimulation, for example, as in the Ganzfeld. One study showed that a group experiencing one week in PD conditions produced more reports of loss of contact with reality and changes in body image than a similar group in SD or an ambulatory control group.

Sensory deprivation is a universal experience in one form or another. It is not only present in research experiments but can be experienced in sleep, highway hypnosis, entrapment in mines or caves, extended space travel and by jet pilots, shipwrecked crews, lost explorers, prisoners in solitary confinement, self-exiled recluses or mystics. Indefinite bomb shelter confinement is only one contemporary possibility where one may need to cope with prolonged sensory deprivation.

The Inuit (or Eskimo) of West Greenland faces severe sensory deprivation reactions almost as a way of life. These reactions are called "kayak-angst" and are regarded as a national disease. The male hunters out alone on a calm, mirror-like body of water with a glaring sun overhead, staring down into the water and making minimal and repetitive movements, soon lose consciousness to some extent along with external reference points for stable perception. Cognitive distortions and impaired judgments create confusion and dizziness. Physical distortions follow, such as the idea that the kayak is filling up with water, but the hunter is afraid to move in the small craft in order to reassure himself and get comfortable. A form of trance ensues. Some hunters refuse to go out alone because of this syndrome. West Europeans in similar circumstances report experiences of feeling themselves distant from their bodies, whereas the Inuit seldom give such reports. People such as the relatively less emotional Truk Islanders are virtually unaffected by this type of extreme isolation.

The Trukese people, of South Pacific origin, have less

concern for self or the future and no psychological dependence on time. Therefore, they can take 200-mile ocean voyages in a canoe without severe psychological stress or despair when they become lost at sea. Small familial crews set out on these long journeys knowing what to expect from past experience and having a fairly clear idea of what to do and what not to do. The psychological reaction of a crew of European sailors with no past experience at being lost at sea is much more traumatic. So, one's preparation for deprivation experiences shapes one's reaction to them to some extent.

However, kayak-angst reactions persist despite the Eskimo's familiarity with the experience and his ability to predict reactions due to prior exposure. Kayak-angst will actually increase in intensity or frequency, or both, and terminate only in drowning or abandoning hunting altogether. Here we have a phenomenon with variable reactions and insufficient explanation. Whereas past history may be seen to explain the difference in reaction between Truk and European sailors, basic psychological defense structures seem to account for differences between the Truk and Inuit, or Eskimo, experiences. The Eskimo's basic defense is self-withdrawal, exemplified by a high rate of suicide. Truk people lack a strong concept of self and intense feelings are often suppressed if not repressed. Whereas a lost Caucasian may make notches on a boat to indicate last contact with known conditions, at a certain point in time when all hope is considered lost, the personality begins to break down. Trukese would never reach this point because they do not pay strict attention to time of day or date. They merely consider seasonal changes and the coming and going of light for their daily routines.

What has this to do with OBE? Where there is not a strong concept of self or where the basic psychological defense mechanism is withdrawal in face of stress, or where one is accustomed to adverse conditions and unperturbed by them, OBES are not reported. In similar types of sensory deprivation where one is unaccustomed to the surroundings and has a strong sense of self, which fears extinction and knows no way out of the dilemma but is not consciously willing merely to withdraw psychologically, one may experience the self as alive and well and at a safe distance from the disaster. This sort of evidence seems to corroborate both the narcissistic and immortality theories considered earlier in this chapter.

Anthropologist Erika Bourguignon has done extensive research on altered states of consciousness, especially those of dreams, trance, and spirit possession. Some discussion of spirit possession seems necessary in this book since people have been just as concerned that someone might get into their bodies as they have with the idea that they could get out. This phenomenon, as well as OBEs, has been reported throughout the ages across cultures. Both types of phenomena must be considered not only from the point of view of individual psychological functioning, but also from that of societal functioning. Bourguignon states:

> Since trancelike states can be produced in animals by restricting their field of attention, we may easily accept the capacity for ... dissociation, as a part of man's psychobiological heritage.... Where dissociational experiences are valued, techniques for inducing them often exist. These techniques again vary widely, from the breathing patterns of whirling dervishes ... to the use of drugs ... to the use of music, dance, or certain herbs.[17]

There is an obvious continuity of motivation in both spirit possession and OBE. That is, when people choose to come back to the body or out of the trance, they do so. Spirit possession, however, exhibits a discontinuity of memory and personal identity not usually present in OBEs. Bourguignon believes this type of amnesia serves a valuable purpose.

> While dissociations do in fact entail discontinuity of the self, in the sense of personal identity, memory, and responsibility, may they not be thought of as *enlarging* the field of action of the self, rather than restricting it? [For example, in dissociated states, one may experience access to healing powers, which are inaccessible in normal states of consciousness.] Can we not speak here indeed of "dissociation in the service of the self," much as Ernest Kris (1952) speaks of "regression in the service of the Ego?"
> ... [R]itualized dissociation provides the self with an alternate set of roles, in addition to his everyday inventory of roles, in which unfulfilled desires, "unrealistic" in the context of the workaday world, get a second chance at fulfillment, a fullfillment which is surely not merely vicarious because the glory goes to the possessing spirit rather than to the "horse."
> ... In a world of poverty, disease, and frustration, ritual possession, rather than destroying the integrity of the self, provides increased scope for fulfillment.[18]

M.J. Field studied spirit possession in Ghana[19] and found a marked slowing down as the first phase of possession. This is reminiscent of Harary's "cooling down" period prior to OBE. The second phase of possession is a burst of energy. Both the beginning and end of the excited phase are abrupt.

At times the possessed person performs incredible feats of strength and endurance. This may be possible because of a lack of self-observation and restraint. Some drop dead from exhaustion whereas others rise out of deathbeds to move and dance with incredible motor activity. It appears the mind has recesses of memory and judgment that may be closed to normal consciousness but accessible in possession as well as in out-of-body states.

Lee observed spirit possession among the Zulu[20] with a basic question in mind, "Why do certain people become possessed?" Anthropologists give explanations in terms of stress in the social order and the acquisition of greater status through possession. Psychiatrists see manifestations of psychopathological states, frequently of a hereditary character.

Earlier in this chapter, it was stated that febrile-toxic states of typhus and influenza often predispose individuals to autoscopic experiences. In Lee's study we find that two of the most serious epidemics in Zulu history (influenza in 1919/20 and malaria in 1933) were among the causes of the rapid spread of ancestor-possession, which is directed at curing illness. It appears the Zulu saw many friends and relatives dying and society's not being able to help them, so they reached out for any help or comfort they felt might be available. I see nothing psychopathological about taking such a position.

Women among the Zulu seem to have a special vested interest in spirit possession. There is a seven-to-one preponderance of women diviners. For a Zulu woman in 1950, to become a diviner was the only culturally recognized way of winning general social prestige. As early as 1943, the Zulu women said their possessions were a reaction to neglect or to the dullness of women's lives. By becoming the center of trance possession rituals, and by forcing their relatives to give them occasional feasts, they hoped to attract attention and enliven their existence. A male homosexual may also find acceptance through becoming a diviner. So, people who are despised by their society, such as in some cases women or homosexuals, may find a means of acceptance through possession.

Mischel and Mischel[21] found that spirit possession, like

any other behavior, is perpetuated only if it is in some way rein-
forcing or rewarding to those who exhibit it (positive or negative
reinforcement).

The practice of spirit possession permits the sanctioned
expression of behaviors otherwise socially unacceptable or
unavailable. The personal transition is often an almost direct role
reversal—from passive impotence to central importance,
dominance, power, and recognition, which appear to be the
major reinforcements obtained through this behavior pattern.
(Not everyone gets reinforced in this way; some are faced with
ridicule and rejection when they attempt to gain such stature
under possession.) Spirit possession has two major positively rein-
forcing general functions.

Its first such function is in supplying an available, socially
sanctioned (at least within the practicing group) framework for
the interpretation and acceptance of otherwise threatening and
disturbing phenomena, such as unusual psychological or physical
symptoms. Example: Where hysterical symptoms develop, the
afflicted person or those around him or her, while under
possession, seem to interpret these symptoms as the first signs of a
special gift. This not only prevents the deviation from becoming
a source of social stigma but, on the contrary, makes it a valued
behavior, regardless of the ultimate personal consequences. The
belief system that can change behavior otherwise considered a
malignant symptom into one that is prized and reinforced is itself
reinforced by the process.

Second, the practice of spirit possession is rewarding as it
permits reference of virtually all serious problems to the
"powers" for solution. Thereby, the individual is to some degree
freed of responsibility for controlling and directing his or her
own life. This not only gives aid in difficult decisions but also
alleviates anxiety about such choices. Problems are not given
over to some "outside power." The power to which they are
transferred is directly and personally experienced within the participant's own body and, although not credited as such by the
possessed, is an extension as it were of the individual's conscious
behavior. That is, the power is an aspect of the individual,
presumably without awareness, which emerges during
possession.

Many Western psychiatrists and clinical psychologists
give short shrift to these basic human experiences that have trans-

forming effects on people's lives. They seem to be content in making up new names for the experience and putting it into syndromes. They do not seem to be trying to help people consciously integrate the meaning of the experience into their daily lives. Detaching emotionally and becoming an objective observer of one's experience as in an OBE, however momentary or mundane, would seem to me a legitimate psychological goal.

As I said earlier, profound attitude changes concerning life and death are often a result of depersonalization-type experiences. Meaning and direction are also given to the life of the individual who participates in spirit possession. As one leader put it: "Being a Shango woman is my life."

End Notes

[1]D. Scott Rogo, "Aspects of Out-of-the-Body Experiences," *Journal of the Society for Psychical Research* 48 (1976):329-335.

[2]L.E. Hinsie and R.J. Campbell, *Psychiatric Dictionary*, 4th ed. (New York: Oxford University Press, 1970), p. 200.

[3]John C. Nemiah, "Depersonalization Neurosis," in *Comprehensive Textbook of Psychiatry — II*, eds. A. Freedman, H. Kaplan, and B. Sadock (Baltimore: Williams & Wilkins, 1975), p. 1268.

[4]*Ibid.*, p. 1270.

[5]*Ibid.*, p. 1271.

[6]Mortimer Ostow, "The Metapsychology of Autoscopic Phenomena," *International Journal of Psychoanalysis* 41 (1960):619-625.

[7]Caro W. Lippman, "Hallucinations of Physical Duality in Migraine," *Journal of Nervous and Mental Disease* 117 (1953):345-350. Experiences of eight migraine patients are discussed. OBES are classified as hallucinations even though the patient considers the "second body" more real and in control of mental qualities such as observation, judgment, and perception. Very interesting report.

[8]J. Todd and K. Dewhurst, "The Double: Its Psychopathology and Psycho-Physiology," *Journal of Nervous and Mental Disease* 122 (1955):47-55. Discusses specific and predisposing factors facilitating the appearance of a visual hallucination of the self.

[9]D.J. Lyle, *Neuro-Ophthalmology*, 1945.

[10]Bollea, *Rivista di Neurología* 18 (1948):337.

[11]Kenneth Dewhurst, "Autoscopic Hallucinations," *Irish Journal of Medical Science* (1954):263-267.

[12]Heinz E. Lehmann, "Unusual Psychiatric Disorders and Atypical Psychoses," in *Comprehensive Textbook of Psychiatry — II*,

eds. A. Freedman, H. Kaplan, and B. Sadock (Baltimore: Williams & Wilkins, 1975), pp. 1727-1728.

[13]R.K. Siegel, "The Psychology of Life after Death," *American Psychologist* 35:10 (October 1980):911-931.

[14]Russell Noyes, Jr., and D.J. Slymen, "The Subjective Response to Life-Threatening Danger, *Omega* 9:4 (1978-1979):313-321.

[15]Karlis Osis and Donna McCormick, "Insiders' Views of the OBE," *ASPR Newletter* 4:3 (July 1978):9.

[16]J.P. Zubek, ed., *Sensory Deprivation: Fifteen Years of Research* (New York: Appleton-Century-Crofts, 1969).

[17]Erika Bourguignon, "The Self, the Behavioral Environment and the Theory of Spirit Possession," in *Context and Meaning in Cultural Anthropology*, ed. M.E. Spiro (New York: Free Press, 1965), p. 42.

[18]*Ibid.*, pp. 55, 57.

[19]M.J. Field, "Spirit Possession in Ghana," in *African Mediumship and Society*, eds. J. Beattie and J. Middleton (New York: Africana Publishing, 1970).

[20]S.G. Lee, "Spirit Possession among the Zulu," in *African Mediumship and Society*, eds. J. Beattie and J. Middleton (New York: Africana Publishing, 1970).

[21]W. Mischel and F. Mischel, "Psychological Aspects of Spirit Possession," *American Anthropologist* 60 (1958):249-260.

Chapter VIII

Whoever Said You Were
In the Body Anyway?

Thomas Alva Edison once said, "We know less than one millionth of one percent about anything." On the assumption that this is true, why do we think we are inside our bodies anyway?

Some cultures hold the belief that people function from their hearts; our culture seems to hold the belief that we function from inside our brains or heads. If the living entity can be thought of as being located in the heart or brain, is it not just as easy to think of it as outside the body — operating the body from a foot above the head or any other location that feels right?

Philosophical materialists adhere to the idea that we are in bodies and therefore identical with them. Many theories have been put forward as to how the mind and body are interrelated. Present-day philosopher Michael Grosso suggests as a possible conceptualization of the mind-body problem that one "*always was out of the body* and that the paranormal OBE represents one type of empirically dramatic and self-certifying instance of becoming fully conscious of the fact."[1]

Another philosopher, C.J. Ducasse, concluded twenty years ago that "the soul is not in the body, but the body is in, and dependent upon, the soul, which precedes and survives it, and whose force gives form and organization to the matter of which the body is composed."[2]

Some research seems to show that one can obtain extrasensory information more readily when the body is inert and the field of consciousness associated with it is allowed to drift aimlessly. Altered states of consciousness, such as dreaming or those produced by Ganzfeld techniques, have been seen to be psi-

76

conducive states. Likewise with OBES, we may not need to get out of our bodies but just get our bodies out of the way as through sleep, hypnosis, meditation, or other altered states.

A mystic or yogi sitting in perfect physical stillness, systematically withdrawing attention from external stimulation, sometimes reports experiencing universal freedom. Swami Satchidananda stated that our belief that we are identical with our bodies is contradicted by our language. If we are in the body and identical with it, why do we use the possessive "my" when we speak of it? We speak of it as something we own, not something we are. With our belief that we are in the body, it would be more appropriate to say, "I hurt up here," than our usual comment that "my head hurts."

People's experiences during OBES range from feeling they have an identical phantom body to feeling that they are a point of light some distance removed from the body. Thus, it is possible to experience oneself in a specific location in a body (heart, head, and so forth), or in a phantom body, or as a nonsubstantive point of consciousness. One might experience great difficulty moving a few feet from the body as an out-of-body entity or one might seem instantly transported hundreds of miles with no apparent means of navigation, experiencing being not only outside the body but also outside the force of gravity. One may experience different degrees of density of the out-of-body entity as well as degrees of voluntary control over the experience. The OBE is not an all-or-nothing phenomenon, but operates on a continuum of varying degrees of feeling more or less free of the physical organism.

One theory of why we believe that we are in the body is that it gives us psychological security. Though ordinarily true, it would be false in times of possible destruction, when we might find security in feeling separated from the endangered physical body. Spontaneous experiences often occur when the body is in grave physical danger, as in accidents, major operations, or illnesses. They may occur when one is under extreme emotional strain and has a great need to be at another place in order to relieve anxiety. Extraordinary fatigue can also bring the experience about spontaneously.

Most people seem to believe that the only reality is that which they can see, taste, touch, smell, or hear. By making this assumption, they logically move to the conclusion that they *are* their senses or physical bodies. Operating within this belief system, they should believe that if the body were destroyed, they would no longer exist. But in fact at this point a contradiction in their thought processes seems to occur. According to a Gallup poll, 73 per cent of Americans do accept as reality the concept of life after death. In a sociological poll by Greeley, 27 per cent of the American population "feel as though they were really in touch with someone who had died."[3] That's more than 50,000,000 people! The belief system shifts when the thought of death enters the picture whether due to experience, or "gut feelings," or fear of nonexistence, and this assumption that identifies consciousness with the body crumbles.

Because we seem to hold onto our bodies for "dear life," one might think that the belief systems as reported in the polls merely reflect lip service to an ideal. However, Karlis Osis in his cross-cultural studies of experiences at the time of death has found that fear is by no means the dominant emotion at the moment of death. In fact, an opposite emotion — peace — is often experienced. This suggests that in the final act of transition, our "lip service" belief system does seem to be accepted and maintained.

Is it possible that it threatens one's sanity to suspect that one can operate independently of the body? People may be afraid they are going out of their minds, when they are actually only going out or experiencing being out of their bodies. Just as personalities are multifaceted, reality is multidimensional and experienced on different levels at different times.

For example, a conversion experience may be sensed at first by heart palpitations, tremors, or a sensation of lightness, but no one can deny the reality of the personality and behavior transformation that often comes about as a result of such an experience. Because people rely so heavily on their sense perceptions, they often exclude or deny other types of awareness. Some deny the power of conversion experiences and condemn intuitive insights as wishful thinking. The value and importance of spiritual and intuitive experiences are underestimated in our verbal- and sensory-dominated society.

We are educated, and sometimes even threatened at an early age, not to believe in anything other than sense-related phenomena. For instance, imaginary playmates are imaginary, *not* real. By the same token, you could not have gone to grandmother's house one night while you were asleep — no matter how convincing the evidence — because it is "impossible." The "impossibility" may not be in the doing of these things, but in the realization that they were done.

People sometimes report drug-related OBES. Some drugs alter perception, behavior, and concepts such as where one is localized in space. Chemicals introduced into our systems may change our moods, attitudes, and even our ability to operate our bodies correctly. They may affect our memories and cause us to perceive our external environment differently. These are called mind-altering drugs, but what they are actually altering are neurohumoral substances that transmit electrochemical impulses across synapses in the brain. When the transmitter substances are changed or suppressed, sense perceptions change — as do our actions and reactions to them. Operation of the physical body is affected. Whether the "operator" is affected or not is undetermined. For instance, if your car were out of gas, it would not affect your ability to drive; you just couldn't get the car started.

Large portions of human brain cortex have been damaged, removed, or anesthetized without the patient's losing consciousness and without mental impairment. Brain research workers continue to try to localize higher intellectual processes. They observe an invulnerability of memory and general intellectual capacity to large amounts of brain damage in some cases. Higher brain function appears to be diffused over a large portion of the brain with many duplicate or redundant operations and connections. Faculties such as movement, speech, or hearing may be affected, but patients are often still apparently able to think and handle their mental affairs. A partially paralyzed body does not necessarily limit cognitive processing. Can our true essence be identical with the brain, if this is true? The mind or mental life is independent of the brain in these examples. If one can conceive of mind as being independent within the body, then it may be possible to realize mind's independence in space.

Experiential reports confirm again and again that people are sometimes aware in comas, are cognitively intact despite brain damage, can think and feel as clearly and strongly as ever with a paralyzed body, and even watch resuscitation attempts on their bodies when they have been declared "clinically dead." It is difficult to comprehend how we continue to hold the belief that we are limited to a body or permanently encased in one in view of countless reports to the contrary from many different cultures throughout the centuries.

Human bodies are developed in such a way as to ensure life in present circumstances (as in the womb) and life in future conditions. In other words, the body is not formed solely according to the environment in which it first exists. So, a fetus grows lungs it will use at some later time, as well as eyes, ears, vocal chords, and so forth. Later in life one grows a second set of teeth and some people even start on a third. It is fascinating to entertain the idea that perhaps at this moment, systems are being constructed within us to cope with future conditions.

Minds are connected with bodies, but the mind that operates the body seems to be unaware of how the body was created or even exactly how it works in minute detail. We know that if we make a decision to raise our hand, we raise our hand but we have no idea of the physical complexity involved in that movement. We take it for granted that we know how we move our bodies just as we take it for granted that we are inside them.

There are many theories as to the mind-body relation that involve ideas of materialism and mechanism. Some would imply that a series of brain actions causes thought. Quantum physicists are beginning to view the physical world as consisting basically of interactions, of indivisible processes — not just as individual particles of matter in space and time — but *as* ongoing, immeasurable interactions. On the quantum level of analysis, ordinary laws of cause and effect, exact probability, and determinism break down.

Even to observe a physical event at the quantum level is to affect it. This is not unlike the "experimenter effects" found in both psychological and parapsychological studies. The implication is that mind, or the conscious act of observing alone, actively influences the physical event that is being observed. There are laws stating the probability that a specific interaction *might* occur, but on the quantum level it is by definition impossible to say when or whether it *will* occur: Only the probability of occurrence of the event is determined, not the occurrence of the event itself. That is, one can predict a future event to be highly probable, but it may not in fact occur. Events do not follow one another in a mechanical, causal sequence, and the mere act of observation can alter the flow of events in physically indeterminable ways.

It is important to realize that the brain is constructed in such a way that its action is in some ways more properly described by the noncausal, nonmechanic quantum laws rather than by the causal, mechanistic laws that are useful at a macroscopic level of analysis. On this basis it becomes easier to consider the possibility that mind or thought is not produced by the action of the brain, but rather that mind may be something that can operate the brain much as a computer operator uses a computer. The mind may therefore not necessarily be located in the brain although it may interact with it, or focus through it in greater or lesser degree. If the mind is not located in the brain, it would be free to operate in other places as well and one would expect phenomena such as OBES to occur — as apparently they do.

There is freedom for thought in a double-aspect theory of mind and body as coexistent and interacting, but neither necessarily caused by the other. The body seems necessary for operation within physical reality, but it is our experience as we know it that is the fundamental truth of our being.

To say one obtains another point of view in space during an OBE is to imply that consciousness is in space. However, since time and space are concepts that provide some order to daily physical existence, it is probably more likely that in an OBE we obtain another point of view *of* space. Once again, it is perhaps not the experience that is lacking but the realization, acceptance, and correct interpretation of it. It is so tempting to take all these ideas for granted rather than trying to think them through from our own physical and intuitive experience. That is, it is not necessary and could be erroneous to believe at face value that we are in bodies or even in space. My experience suggests that I can control a body (at least while awake) and perceive space but am not limited by either of them.

Any time a psychic event occurs, the human being appears to transcend time and space dependencies. Humans may experience many levels of reality, which may assume different appearances, without necessarily changing their own personal identities. Analogously, music may be sung, played on an instrument, heard on the radio, exist in the form of sound waves or preserved on a record or tape, or felt as a sensual, emotional, or intellectual experience. Its appearance does not alter its essence — it will always be the same music — but one's perception of it changes. Psychic research has established that space and time may be transcended and that humanity possesses within itself powers inexplicable by mechanistic science.

Establishment science is threatened by the existence of psi phenomena. If OBES and other so-called paranormal events are taken seriously, almost every branch of knowledge will undergo drastic fundamental changes. Cherished theories do not die easily and rethinking entire conceptual frameworks thought to be sound is laborious in the extreme. Carrington suggested more than 30 years ago that a whole new system of human thought will have to be born, which affirms that "life and mind are as real as matter and motion, and that the human spirit is, after all, worthy of a dignified and respected place" in all scientific endeavors.[4]

There are a few findings from scientific laboratories that bear on the issue of brain-mind relations and the following is just one example. Deecke, Scheid, and Kornhuber[5] did some interesting neurophysiological experiments that relate to the mind-body problem. Their 16 subjects were asked to lie on a table, relaxing, and spontaneously flex their right index fingers more than 200 times irregularly, preferably without memory of the last movement. Most subjects did two or three experiments although some subjects participated in up to ten experiments. Finger muscle movements and brain electrical activity were recorded and computerized.

If the brain alone moved the finger, action should be directed from motor pyramidal cells in the motor cortex to the finger and we would realize the movement only after it occurred. However, when one decides or remembers to move the right finger, the first event about .8 of a second preceding a movement of the finger is not an electrical potential over the left motor cortex but rather something called a readiness potential. This is a firing of nerve cells widely spread over the surface of the brain. At a little less than .1 of a second before movement, there is another widespread potential. At 1/20 of a second before movement, a motor potential is activated in the left motor cortex.

In other words, when a decision is made to move one's finger, neurons begin to fire over a large area of the surface of the brain. About .7 of a second later, they center in on the specific motor cells that move the right index finger.

The researchers also asked subjects to repeatedly say the

word "Lotte." Speech is a more complicated cognitive process than muscle movement, and it takes 1.5 seconds of readiness potential before the word is spoken.

Sir John C. Eccles, neuroscientist and Nobel Laureate in Medicine, considers this work of primary importance to the mind-body problem and concludes from these studies:

> I do believe that the mind has its own existence, its own independence, apart from the brain. It works intimately with the brain, but it is superior to the brain. It wasn't something from the brain that gave me the feeling I had the intention to move my finger; it came from the mind. And this is, I think, essential to any understanding of human action and responsibility.[6]

And Carrington again speaks to us out of the past: the human body "is supposed not only to run itself, but to initiate original ideas and to perpetuate other machines like itself *ad infinitum*. The dogma of mechanism, carried to its logical conclusion, ends in absurdity."[7]

Modern methods of communication have brought the ideas of prominent thinkers together to allow for scientific advancement. Ethical and spiritual advancement is slow in comparison. As more scientists turn their laboratories to the study of spiritual forces and factors, I believe we will see more advancement in one generation than we have in the past four. Adopting a self-image of humans as beings rather than "just" bodies would have a tremendous impact on the way we relate to one another and the universe. It could bring a wholly new concept of reality, based on fact, which would transform behavior rapidly and spontaneously. Is it necessary to wait until we leave the physical world permanently before we can appreciate currently unknown, invisible realms? Such extremes should not be necessary in our present age of enlightenment. New understanding can emerge through realizing that one can become more aware but cannot create awareness in plastic bodies and brains. C.D. Broad's experiences with the famous medium Gladys Osborne Leonard helped liberate his logic to the point that he suggested, "one human body *need not* be connected with only one self."[8]

What is our stake in refusing to believe that we can operate independently of the body? Why is it okay to know that we are spiritual beings, but not okay to know that we can move around invisibly at will? Our old ethical problem rears its ugly head again: If we could do these things, wouldn't we use them for destructive means? The media certainly suggest this is the only way we would use them. The only way I can see to bridge this gap is to begin to learn constructive uses for our psychic abilities. My parents did not keep me from walking or tell me that I couldn't, even though they knew I might accidentally walk in front of a moving vehicle; they did teach me how to cross the street safely.

End Notes

[1]Michael Grosso, "Some Varieties of Out-of-Body Experience," *Journal of the American Society for Psychical Research* **70** (1976):179-183. In this article he discusses the mind-body problem and some states of consciousness in which one feels "out of body."

[2]C.J. Ducasse, *A Critical Examination of the Belief in a Life After Death* (Springfield, Ill.: Thomas, 1961), p. 81.

[3]Andrew M. Greeley, *The Sociology of the Paranormal: A Reconnaissance* (Beverly Hills, Calif.: Sage Publications, 1975), p. 36.

[4]Hereward Carrington, *The Invisible World* (Philadelphia: Ruttle, Shaw & Wetherill, 1946), p. 148.

[5]L. Deecke, P. Scheid, and H.H. Kornhuber, "Distribution of Readiness Potential, Pre-motion Positivity and Motor Potential of the Human Cerebral Cortex Preceding Voluntary Finger Movements," *Experimental Brain Research* **7** (1969):158-168.

[6]John C. Eccles, "The Human Person in Its Two-Way Relationship to the Brain," in *Research in Parapsychology, 1976*, eds. J.D. Morris, W.G. Roll, and R.L. Morris (Metuchen, N.J.: Scarecrow Press, 1977), pp. 258-259.

[7]Carrington, *The Invisible World*, p. 9.

[8]C.D. Broad, *The Mind and Its Place in Nature* (New York: Harcourt, Brace, 1925), p. 16.

Chapter IX

Social and Ethical Considerations

If we fail to realize or experience that we are traveling in space at this very moment through the Milky Way galaxy at 43,000 miles per hour and around the sun at a speed of 66,600 miles per hour, on a planet wobbling and rotating on its axis one revolution per day, and yet we can stand right out on top of the earth with nothing holding us down but an invisible force of gravity, is it not possible that there are other profound, yet subtle, phenomena that occur without our conscious knowledge?

Western civilization seems to exist within a pattern of experience that cuts us off from most spiritual knowledge. In the case of out-of-body experiences, they could be common unconscious experiences merely awaiting our conscious recognition and acknowledgment. The nature of our mobility in dreams and reports that dreams can sometimes be converted by the dreamer into conscious OBES suggest this possibility.

The United States was founded by a minority who held nontraditional religious and spiritual ideas. Our current national self-image is that of a reasonable, industrious, and efficient technological society. Our well meaning Judeo-Christian practices are often more social or political than spiritual. I feel it is the responsibility of our religious leaders to keep their congregations informed of major social problems and to ask them for prayer and help in these circumstances. However, ecstatic religious practices have been abandoned by some churches in favor of programs that lend social respectability and visibility. As our Western society has "progressed" from simple to complex, ecstatic experiences have been devalued as naive, uneducated, or delusional.

85

How many churches today advocate supernatural inspiration or "getting the spirit"? Some churches still reluctantly maintain a ritual of exorcism to rid parishioners of demonic possessions and destructuve poltergeists. Other churches are somewhat discredited for using various means of altered states of consciousness in faith healing. Speaking in tongues (glossolalia) is only one spiritual "gift" that can still be found in some present-day churches in metropolitan centers, as well as rural communities.

Are churches satisfying the basic spiritual needs of the people? Or are some people driven to seek refuge in one group or another, or in communes, or in shared living space and working spaces of every description in order to feel a sense of belonging? Some of these people may be seeking immediate gratification in every area of life, including ecstatic states, in order to confirm their own beliefs in their personal worth.

In the face of world problems such as poverty, resource shortages, overpopulation, famine, and environmental degradation, why would one want to devote their time and attention to understanding OBES? What could it accomplish to go out of one's body? How can this possibly help us handle our problems any better? Before we can handle any of our life situations effectively, it seems of vital importance to know our potential and capabilities.

If we continue to identify ourselves as bodies, we lose the essence of our scope of abilities. Most social ills derive from the fact that we identify ourselves as separate bodies. Bigotry pervades every aspect of social life and degrades personal interaction. It exists on every level: mental, spiritual, and physical. Perhaps bigotry will not be necessary to boost our faltering egos when we appreciate the spark of life that each of us expresses in myriad ways and our unity with all life forms. As we realize our immaterial personal existence, maybe prejudices — intellectual elitism, religious or spiritual superiority, nationalism concerning the countries in which our bodies were born, whom and what we know, racism or what color our skin is, sexism or whether we are in a male or female body, even what accent, language or dialect we speak — can be considered valuable differences expanding all human experience. Then it will not be necessary to use ideas about our bodies to make one person appear better than anyone else.

Bigotry is ubiquitous and is heightened by our belief that we are bodies and that this facet of existence is the primary one. We describe ourselves as "human beings"; human is the adjective, beings, the noun. So, first we are beings, and beyond consideration for adequate food, clothing, and shelter for our bodies, it might be wise to place our attention on nonmaterial goals to aid human evolution and perhaps spiritual revolution.

If our only experience is in a body, we may well continue to believe that we are a body. If one were born and raised entirely in an automobile, it might have its advantages, but one would never know the joys of being outdoors and feeling the cool grass or warm sunlight directly on the skin. It seems certain that granted the ability to get out of the car just once, one would want to do it again and again to exercise new-found experiences and freedom. From numerous reports, OBES are also freeing experiences in which people realize that they can transcend self-limiting concepts, with more abilities, with more freedom entailing more ethical responsibility, and with an actual awareness of themselves for the first time as beings rather than bodies. This is no longer a belief; for some it is knowledge.

A large majority of people report no fear of death after OBES. Imagine what the release of this basic fear could mean to anyone's life. There are times during life when we have to part with beloved friends because of circumstances beyond our control, or with once-cherished belongings that have become cumbersome, but we cling to our bodies to the extent of even identifying ourselves as the bodies we possess. Why is this so? Of course, the body is a magnificent possession making it possible for us to function visibly and should therefore be cared for and used wisely. But, what control do we have over our bodies? We can put different types of food into it and different articles of clothing on it. We can move it from one place to another, as well as move other objects with it. We can admit light through the iris of the eye and derive pictures out of light and shaded places. Possibly our brain acts as a filing system for past memories and therefore a guiding system for future action. We can admit sound waves and our auditory system can construct meaningful messages out of those waves. Likewise, our consciousness can use the senses of taste, touch, and smell for creating impressions about our physical experience. We use the body in many ways for getting and storing information, experiencing sensations, and to express

our thoughts and feelings to others through orderly and system-
atized communication procedures. The body is a marvelous and
priceless piece of equipment that we can use any way we choose.
That, in itself, is a powerful cognition because we can then
choose how we shall use it, rather than letting others choose for
us or following after blind sensation. (One might speculate from
occult-type literature that there is a great spiritual demand for
bodies and that each of us is indeed fortunate to have one.)

One has relatively little control over the body, considering its demands on the human being. It tells us when and
what to eat to keep it in operation. It tells us to sleep lest it mal-
function. It tells us we need all sorts of physical gratifications,
first one and then another. It places limitations on everything we
can know because it tells us we can go only so far so fast and take
in only so much information or substance at one time. Our sensory systems are screening devices with strict limitations as to
what must be admitted for processing.

Why can we not transcend this demanding and equally
limiting creation and experience life through pure conscious
awareness? We probably feel our body cannot operate without
our presence, but it carries on fine when our consciousness is
temporarily absent in sleep. Persons in coma have recovered after
hundreds of days of unconsciousness. These facts should give us
the idea that we may be able to take a momentary vacation from
our bodies without any serious or damaging effects.

How much do we know about the body's operation
anyway and how much do we actually control? Do we direct
food through proper channels for digestion, distribution,
assimilation, and so forth once we have put it in our mouths and
chewed it? Do we direct the intake of oxygen into the blood-
stream and consciously circulate it to all points of the body? Do
we know how to fire one motor neuron in a specific muscle that
contributes to our ability to move? In this and many other ways,
the body can do very well on its own. It is our spiritual insecurity
that causes us to cling to the body.

Inadequate knowledge of our true nature probably keeps
us bound to a concept of being in a body we can see and therefore
think we know about. As human consciousness evolves, we find
that those who have achieved what R.M. Bucke[1] called cosmic
consciousness bring us the message of our unity with all life. A
body seems not to be in unity with all life by reason of its ap-

parent material structure and boundaries. However, a unitive experience may emerge from a consideration that bodies are moving masses of atoms spinning at certain frequencies in a fluidic universal energy field. Mystics have repeatedly affirmed that we are not bodies, but that we possess bodies. There is great freedom and liberation in knowing this.

Unlike animals, people are self-conscious and they usually identify the self with that which seems most alive, real, or intense. Some are identified with their bodies, experiencing and often talking about themselves mainly in terms of sensations. Some are identified with their feelings. Others are identified with their thinking processes and even describe feelings in intellectual terms expressing little or no emotion. Many are identified with a role and live, function, experience, and define themselves as the role, such as husband, mother, student, executive, or teacher. Being identified with only a part of one's personality hampers the ability to identify with other parts, to enjoy them, and utilize them to their full potential. As one realizes these self-imposed limitations, one may become frustrated and be tormented by painful feelings of inadequacy, insecurity, and failure. However, this realization can also be the impetus for expanded awareness of one's being and fuller expression of that life force. Despair is often a trigger for a transforming experience.

Being identified with a body presents devastating problems as one loses physical strength or beauty through age or accident. Being identified with a role produces equally harrowing situations as children eventually leave home, students graduate, and executives are retired. At these times, a fuller understanding of one's essence can facilitate natural evolution into correct identification and more satisfactory personal self-expression. One can operate through a role or a body then, without being identified with it or limited to it.

You are an observer which creates and directs. The observer is not what is observed, created, or directed. The observer has a body but is not merely a body. The observer cares for the body and values it highly, but never identifies itself as the body. One's true essence could hardly be restricted to fleeting feelings of ecstasy or anger, nor to myriad ideas or thoughts experienced daily. The observer is not limited to any of these partial, temporary states. In freeing oneself from the misconceptions described above, Roberto Assagioli's affirmation is helpful:

I recognize and affirm myself as a center of pure self-awareness and of creative, dynamic energy. I realize that from this center of true identity I can learn to observe, direct, and harmonize all the psychological processes and the physical body. I will to achieve a constant awareness of this fact in the midst of my everyday life, and to use it to help me and give increasing meaning and direction to my life.[2]

Many will be afraid of increased self-knowledge because with additional freedom, there is added responsiblity. Many may be unwilling to discipline themselves to the quietness of mind and powerful focus of attention and intention required for the awareness of OBE perceptions and possibilities. Some may be turned back by the disorientation some report as experienced during an OBE concerning cause and effect, personal identity, and time. One may find the unknowingness created about what was once viewed as reality and the new concept of reality first glimpsed in an OBE too uncomfortable to proceed with experimenting. However, as people become more aware, and many are doing so today, they find that they are not limited to solely functioning within and through a body. The fact that many people have latent abilities in consciousness has been evidenced time and again throughout history.

Some spiritual disciplines warn disciples to avoid the distraction of psychic abilities that may emerge on the path to spiritual evolvement. If you begin to experiment with states of consciousness such as OBE, remember that right attitude, discretion, discipline, and correct training are essential.

To appreciate the essence of personal existence has been a common goal throughout history. Groups and disciplines have sprung up continually advocating self-realization, original creativity, self-actualization, spiritual development, and totally functioning and personally responsible lifestyles and habit patterns. The word responsibility may be seen not merely as a burden, but as a *response* to one's *abilities*. We cannot properly respond to our abilities until we know what those abilities are. When fully appreciated, OBEs may be the kind of evidence so many are seeking concerning their true nature and relationship to the universe.

Ethical behavior can be thought of as reasonable and responsible action that promotes the highest good for the most people. Each of us has a moral or ethical code whether we realize it or not. When we abide by that code, we generally experience health, love, prosperity, and free self-expression. It is when we forget or deny the value of, for example, "doing unto others as we would have them do unto us," that our lives tend to spiral downward into misery and meaningless. Therefore, it is wise to practice good ethics in all our endeavors.

One may not have to experience being out of the body to realize personal freedom and nonphysical essence. But apparently for some, OBES provide knowledge of life and death and the truth of one's being. This kind of knowledge could alter one's daily interactions in a positive and constructive way. Each of us has the capability of being transformed, perhaps instantaneously. Paul wrote to the Romans almost 2,000 years ago to this effect: "Do not be conformed to this world but be transformed by the renewal of your mind..." (Romans 12:2).

If social ills can be seen to derive from the fact that we identify ourselves as separate bodies, then sole concern for the care and maintenance of the body on an individual level may be seen as a basic influence on corporate schemes and government programs which lack concern for human dignity. After all, corporations and governments are really only groups of individuals making decisions and taking actions together. If our attention were shifted from a solitary focus on material and monetary gain to that which would produce the highest good for the most people, perhaps a societal ethic would emerge that would affirm our sense of unity and abundant life. It is possible to realize and manifest such an ideal.

Programs for people that concentrate on food and shelter for the body often degrade the spirit and rob human dignity. Material needs are essential but if the social "good works" stop there, they are not effective in the uplifting of human beings and general elevation of consciousness so that individuals can begin to grow into their true self-expression, inner security, and financial independence.

Universal respect for human rights and personal freedom is essential to our well-being. Until we can achieve a self-image that transcends physical limitations and bodily definitions, we will continue to divide ourselves and lessen our collective strength and never embrace a reverence for life and a self-respect that reaches out to every other person.

End Notes

[1]R.M. Bucke, *Cosmic Consciousness* (Secaucas, N.J.: Citadel Press, 1973). Stories of men who have attained another level of consciousness beyond self-consciousness.

[2]Roberto Assagioli, *The Act of Will* (New York: Penguin Books, 1979), p. 216. Explanations of types, purposes, and uses of will and intention.

Questions and Comments[1]

1. Why can some people touch objects while out of the body and others cannot?

Personal experimenters report that their ability to interact with matter depends on the density of the out-of-body entity. It seems the entity can be more or less substantial on different occasions.

2. Why do some people experience the astral cord (or attachment of second body to physical body)?

The "astral cord" is not reported today nearly as regularly as it was in the past. It may act as a psychological symbol of one's sense of security during the experience. It could exist in a report as a preconceived notion. Or, if the OBE is emerging or "being born" as a conscious human experience, the astral cord could be analogous to a kind of umbilical cord. As the OBE becomes more familiar to us and accepted by us, we may no longer need the cord but allow our out-of-body perception to operate fully independent of the physical body.

3. Are other senses than vision involved in OBEs?

Taste, touch, smell, hearing, feeling of emotions and sensations, and the senses of movement and speed are experienced to varying degrees in different people's experiences. Celia Green reports that about a fourth of the people who have more than one experience can feel temperature.[2]

4. Is seeing a phantom double of yourself the same as an OBE?

It could be a type of OBE. One sometimes defines an OBE by point of view of the observer and under this strict definition, physical viewing of one's double does not qualify. This has been called an autoscopic experience (seeing one's self) and the point of view is from eyes to image.

5. What is the difference between autoscopy and OBE?

Autoscopy is a psychological term meaning to see oneself. This was a topic of interest to some medical practitioners during the 1940s and 1950s. It is hoped they will become interested in the phenomenon again as it seems to be directly related to OBES. The point of view is the definitive difference between the two experiences. In an autoscopic experience one sees from physical eyes to a double in space; in OBE one sees from a location in space that is different from where one's body is located. In medical reports however, experiences were often cited as autoscopic even though the point of view was from space to the physical body. When a physiological correlate (specifically brain localization) could not be definitely ascertained for autoscopic experiences, it seems they ceased to be of interest to the medical profession.

6. Is a flying dream an OBE?

Several out-of-body experimenters suggest that flying dreams could well be unconscious OBES. In your next "flying dream," try to obtain some piece of as-yet-unknown information. If you later verify it, this suggests you may have had an OBE, but if the information is not correct, you probably had a flying dream.

7. Does an OBE invade others' privacy?

Moral considerations seem to operate in hypnotized people since they cannot be made to do that which they consider immoral behavior. Some OBE reports also speak of the impossibility of doing something the individual normally feels is incorrect. So, if you do not invade people's privacy in a physical sense, you probably will not desire to do so when you are invisible.

Ethics are extremely important as we begin to use our psychic abilities. Natural laws work perfectly all the time and it is up to the individual whether they be used for destructive or constructive purposes. One has to take absolute responsibility for one's ethical or unethical behavior and be willing to accept the consequences of one's actions.

8. Can drugs get me there faster?

Some people feel that taking drugs will bring glimpses of other realities, which they can then return to without the aid of drugs. This may be true, but drugs also seem to disorient or confuse some who are not ready for these types of experiences. Therefore, safer ways should be explored. Self-observation and daily desire for expanded awareness will probably allow us to be open enough to spontaneously experience that which we desire and learn the most from it.

9. If I have a spontaneous experience, will I then be able to control the ability to go out of body?

Some people are so disturbed or confused by a spontaneous experience that they never repeat it. Most people who have the experience have it more than once but very few take the time and effort required to get the experience under conscious control. An analogy might be that many children play *Chopsticks*, but few go on to be concert pianists. Daily practice to perfect any natural ability requires effort, time, and sacrifice. One painful aspect of evolving into unknown realms of consciousness can be an isolation from peers and a kind of spiritual loneliness.

10. Do children have more OBEs than adults?

Children have a richer fantasy life than adults and this is probably because of their physical limitations and lack of inhibitions. When children describe experiences adults cannot understand, their reports are usually discounted. We have no way at this time of determining the extent of OBEs in children. Granted that it is difficult to tell where a child's imagination ends and an OBE begins, still some investigation of the report could be made rather than flat denial.

For example, place a target out of the child's reach and ask the child to look at it during the next OBE and tell you what it is. Invalidating reports of children's experiences without any investigation may be tantamount to suppressing inherent abilities.

11. Do OBEs prove survival after death?

Data about OBEs from a book such as *Life After Life* are highly suggestive that a conscious entity survives bodily death.[3] There is no proof at this time of survival of death. If we spent as much money trying to answer this question as we do exploring our universe, we might be able to have the answer in the twenty-first century. (Planetary exploration is done with your tax money. If you would rather that research be done on the question of survival of the human personality, it is important to inform your representatives in the government as to how you want your money spent by them.)

12. Most of the experiencers who write about OBE are men; can women do this, too?

Many women have OBES and report them more readily than men. However, reports from women of intuitive or psychic experiences are frequently not taken as seriously as such reports from men. There are books by women on the subject and countless female reports in print. Today there are women who can see clearly at a distance, even from deep under the ocean, and make correct identifications of things they could not have known through sensory means.

It is more often reported that women see apparitions of projected males than the reverse (excepting the Wilmot and Landau cases) and it puzzles me why this should be so. Is it that women can see subtle form more easily or that they have more difficulty taking on a visible form at a distance?

13. Can I operate my body while exterior to it? For instance, can I talk through my body during an OBE?

It is entirely possible that you are always operating your body from a few feet above your head or some other location. Think about that when you are dancing, on a long, disciplined hike, or floating on water. It is only an idea that we are inside our bodies; there is no solid evidence to substantiate this belief.

In reports of OBES, some can talk through the body while they feel they are a distance away from it, but most experience the body as paralyzed until they return to it.

14. How does one get an inner guide to help them with these experiences?

As you reflect on the possibility of having these experiences, if you feel you will need an inner guide, ask for one. It may only be an aspect of your personality which is less frightened to move into expanded awareness, but spiritual aids are sought in many circumstances and are certainly not unknown to Western civilization. How often we hear, "God help me."

15. Do I need a teacher to learn how to have this experience?

If there is someone in your life who has ethical standards of which you approve and in whom you have complete faith and trust and she or he is aware of and able to have these experiences, discussion with that person may prove beneficial to both of you. So-called teachers who charge money to lead you through guided imagery will be of little use to you in your quest toward psychic liberation. Having a friend who understands these things, will set up targets at a distance for you to identify, and will help you analyze your experiences in order to refine them will be most helpful and you will not have to suffer the spiritual loneliness of those exploring on their own. Beware of anyone who says they can lead you into the truth of these experiences with very little effort. There is a temptation to yield to suggestion because it is easier, but there is a joy in personally understanding and feeling these experiences and not taking anyone else's word for it.

16. How will I know when I am ready for this experience?

It will happen and you will know what happened and no one will ever be able to convince you it did not happen, if we can believe the reports of some to whom it has happened.

17. Is it possible to go out and not be able to get back in the body?

Naturally there is no report from anyone who was not able to get back in the body. Most reports indicate that simply thinking about being in the body, places you there immediately. Personal experimenters at times have reported some difficulties in reentering the body, so it could be rather alarming as you try to bring these experiences under conscious control. Fear of death is the toughest obstacle to overcome in order to temporarily liberate your spirit. It may be comforting to know that an overwhelming majority of people who have had an OBE never fear death again.

18. How far should I try to go in the beginning?

There are no rules for how far one should travel in the beginning. People have wide differences of personal freedom on the physical plane and it is probably true on other levels of existence. Neil Armstrong went to the moon; I do not want to. I know a woman who has never traveled more than ten miles from where she was born; I would not want that either.

Go as far as you feel comfortable. Go where you need to go. Go where you most desire to go. Go to the person you are longing to be with. Go the place you would most like to see.

19. How can I resolve my fears enough to let go?

Self-searching, as well as prayer and meditation, may help dissolve fears that are obstructing your approach to this experience. Getting a correct image of yourself as being able to operate independently from the body and expecting it to happen should also aid you. If your fears persist, it may be a form of inner wisdom telling you this experience is not right for you just now. Listen.

20. Can I go crazy trying to do this?

If you do not know what has happened, you may think you are going crazy, but if you are aware that such things are somewhat common in human experience, you should be able to accept the experience as you would any other altered state of consciousness. If you can accept moving at the speed of thought in a dream, you may be able to experience moving at the speed of thought in the altered state known as OBE.

21. Will my body be possessed by another spirit if I go out of body?

There are no reports of this having happened. People who fear this possibility may want to start their experiments with a short statement or ritual for protection.

22. Do we often have these experiences while we are asleep?

Sylvan Muldoon thinks we go out of our bodies every night in sleep to reenergize our systems. One could consider dreams an unconscious OBES. Getting the body out of the way (in sleep) may be the best way to get out of the body. You might try to maintain some conscious awareness of your experiences in sleep. It will not be easy but it may be rewarding.

23. What is the difference between clairvoyance and out-of-body vision?

Clairvoyance is defined as "clear seeing." A clairvoyant impression is usually seen as a mental image in front of or behind the eyes. There is no sense of having been at the actual scene. The feeling is that an image is received.

24. Are telepathy, clairvoyance, and psychokinesis (PK) components of an OBE?

Most OBE reports indicate that communication with others while out of body is usually telepathic or nonverbal. Fox and others felt that clairvoyance was necessary for correct perception of events distant from the body. For instance, Fox wrote about one proposed astral meeting with a fellow experimenter, "If I had only managed to stay in the dream [which facilitated his

OBE], I could have waited here and have met him if he came; but now, even if he does come, as I am awake I shall not be able to see him, for I am not clairvoyant."[4] Eileen Garrett stated that telepathy, clairvoyance, and precognition all contributed to her successful out-of-body experiment from New York to Newfoundland.

PK may be a kind of sending forth a mental probe to rearrange matter in some way. In Schmeidler's work with Ingo Swann,[5] he reportedly changed the temperature at a distance in this way. He would send forth what he called a "mental probe," supposedly to speed up or slow down molecular activity and thereby change the temperature. This seems like some sort of partial OBE.

25. Is it really safe to try to obtain another viewpoint in space?

The safety in doing OBE experimenting would rely on your mental and emotional stability, motivation, intention, and technique. If, at any time, you feel uncomfortable in any way as a result of doing personal experimentation of this nature, my advice would be to stop trying so hard, have faith in your sense of timing, and be patient with yourself. It appears that when one is ready for this new type of experience, it happens spontaneously and is usually rewarding. Pushing yourself too far too fast may lead to unpleasant experiences or worse yet, delusion.

26. Do you think patients are sometimes diagnosed as schizophrenic when they talk about personal OBEs?

The question is often asked in psychiatric diagnostic interviews, if one has ever felt one's self apart from one's body. I assume that if this question is answered in the affirmative, some sort of opinion is held that you are prone to hallucinatory behavior. I imagine if you suggested that you have been seen by others as an apparition at a distance from your body, or that you had verified perceptions in this condition, or somehow affected a change in the environment at a distance, opinions would probably run to egomania, delusions of grandeur, or possibly schizophrenia.

27. Some people claim that they can read while out of body; has this been demonstrated in labs?

An ability to read letters and numbers while reportedly out of body has not been adequately demonstrated in laboratory situations. Miss Z in Tart's sleep laboratory did correctly identify a five-digit number, but the evidence is not conclusive that this was totally due to exterior vision. Other possibilities include telepathy, clairvoyance, precognition, or subliminal perception. People often claim they can read letters and numbers in spontaneous cases but under controlled conditions this has not been verified to my knowledge.

28. If Swann can only perceive shape, size, and color, does this mean his OBE is a right-hemisphere function?

Ingo Swann's ability to perceive outside of visual range did have the markings of a right-hemisphere function. It has been predicted that ESP processing is localized in the right brain, but no conclusive evidence is available to substantiate this theory. This is a wide open area for future research.

29. What is the best, safest method to induce an OBE?

In the OBE literature, most people advocate trying to bring consciousness to the dream state and launch into an OBE from there. Probably deep desire coupled with an attitude of patient expectation and readiness would also be a good way to proceed. Simple acceptance that it can happen and expectation that it will happen would be a broad leap toward a new concept of reality.

30. Are there different planes or levels you can visit while out of body (for example, Powell's astral, mental, and etheric planes; Monroe's locales; or Lilly's plus and minus states)?

There seems to be a consensus among those who write about OBEs that different conditions and environments can be experienced. These range from pleasant to unpleasant, encountering helpers as well as hinderers, going from total darkness to glaring light, from moving at high velocity to being in a stark stillness, as well as earthlike areas and places that have no resemblance to physical life.

31. Can visualizing the experience help bring it about?

Using visualization in the sense of hypnagogic imagery as suggested by Rogo would seem to be a good method for some. It does not seem one could have a correct visualization of what it would be like to be out of one's body until one has experienced it, therefore visualization techniques without having had the experience may lead to self-deception and preconceived imaginary flights. Once having had the experience, it may be a workable technique to visualize being there again.

32. How can I obtain personal proof that my OBE is real?

When you feel you are out of body, try to ascertain where you are and obtain some otherwise unknown information which you can later personally verify. Or, get a friend to set up targets for you and help analyze and keep track of your success. Study the effects of the experience on your daily life. A real OBE generally produces a profound effect on the experient's life and opinions, especially regarding life after death.

33. How can I get control of this experience?

If you are having spontaneous experiences now, try to bring as much critical faculty to them as possible in order to learn some control over them. Patience and effort are required to perfect any specialized talent. Disciplined practice with specific goals in mind are important on a daily basis. A lot of this work will have to be done alone with very little understanding from those around you so if you can find a friend to explore with you, it will be helpful.

34. Will I always be able to direct where I go once I can repeat the experience at will?

Since you are moving into mysterious and unknown realms of experience, total control would seem to diminish one's possibilities for learning all that one might. Most experimenters who had considerable control over these experiences would sometimes find themselves in unknown areas and baffling circumstances. It would seem that total control is not only an undesirable goal, but an impossible dream.

35. How much is memory involved in verifying the OBE?

If the memory is vague of what was seen in an OBE, verification will be more difficult. One might begin to tune up one's memory by making daily efforts to recall dreams. Without a memory of an experience, it is as if it never happened.

36. Is it possible to direct the OBE to people rather than just places?

Some personal experimenters say that it is easier to direct one's self to a person than a place. There are suggestions that a dynamic target is better than a static one. Blue Harary's experiments with his kittens are a good example of this.[6] There are probably individual differences here and if you are people-oriented in daily life, it may be easier for you to visit a person than a place in an OBE.

37. Will my second body be identical to my physical body?

Your second body may take on any number of different forms. It could well resemble your physical body, but it could just as well be an invisible point of view in space. It could be a ball of light or a misty outline. The manifestation of your second body will perhaps be influenced by whatever you unconsciously conceive it to be.

38. Can one always pass through material objects while out of body?

Density of the out-of-body entity and your personal beliefs about what it can do will perhaps determine your experience to some extent. Therefore, if you do not think that you can pass through a door and the density of your second body is almost identical with your physical body, you may have to open the door in the normal way or be blocked by it. Most claims are that one can pass through matter readily, but manipulate it only rarely.

39. Can I get hurt passing through doors and walls during an OBE?

I know of no reports where people have been injured when passing through matter in an out-of-body state. Sometimes one can feel the sensation of passing through matter, but more often it is done without a thought as if it were the most natural thing to do. Some people are amazed when they discover this can be done so effortlessly.

I have heard reports where the out-of-body entity was moving slightly ahead of the physical body. It would pass through a door easily, but forget to open the door for the body, which was following. The body would then collide into the door. When I bang into something unconsciously, I immediately look to see what I had been thinking just then. I assume it must have been pretty important for me to be so careless with my body.

40. Can one see invisible particles such as atoms or molecules in an OBE?

There are some indications in the literature that some experients report seeing at an atomic level. Swann expressed having difficulty seeing through light rays and certain conditions of ionization. Spontaneous case descriptions of fluidic matter and misty vapors may or may not be perceptions of atomic structure or electromagnetic waves.

41. How long can one stay out of the physical body without doing damage to it?

There is no absolute answer to this question. Extended OBES (hour or more) do seem to tax the body unnecessarily. When you feel strain or excessive effort in your experimentation, stop for awhile. One can probably obtain enough data in a few seconds or moments to have food for thought for days. Moderation is advised in practicing these states. Overdoing any novel, possibly confusing, task will likely lead to exhaustion and disorientation.

42. Are OBEs generally felt to be pleasant or frightening?

One cannot generalize about sensations in an OBE. Sometimes they are reported as extremely pleasant and other times as frightening but most people stress that the experience is unforgettable and has a profound effect on the rest of their lives.

43. Is there a limit on how far away one should go from the physical body?

Some feel safe rising above their body a few feet and some are secure enough to attempt trips into the universe and other unknown regions. Do not overextend yourself but try to practice on a gradient.

44. Will I be able to judge distance and time during an OBE?

Distance and time seem to be somewhat distorted in these experiences. While perception of concrete situations may be accurate, judgment about abstract conditions may be confused. It is often easier to measure a room by walking across it than to judge it from vision alone. Opinions as to time and distance are discrete decisions based on past experience in the physical body.

45. Can I go and see deceased friends and relatives while out of body?

Near-death experiences often include reports of visitations with those who have permanently left the physical world. For instance, one child, on being resuscitated, reported being with her deceased brother. Her mother was amazed because she had never told her daughter about the older brother who had passed away as a child. However in OBES, reports of seeing the dead are infrequent.

46. Will I be able to recognize friends and relatives in other existences?

Some do report being able to visit areas where they meet and recognize friends and relatives. These are only claims and have not been scientifically verified.

47. How can one communicate during OBEs (mentally or verbally)?

From case reports, communication seems to be mental in an OBE. It also appears that the double can sometimes relay information through the physical body (that is, talk while exterior) and there are some reports of being able to hear conversations between humans while out of body.

48. Can one become physically debilitated by practicing OBEs too often?

I have seen cases of persons becoming debilitated from excessive practice. We don't fully understand the energies or effort required to control these experiences and therefore if one overexerts oneself unknowingly, it may cause physical discomfort or exhaustion, or both.

49. Is an OBE generally exhausting or refreshing and exhilarating?

There is no general result of these experiences. Profound effects are sometimes produced within the individual, but they are wide ranging and extremely variable. The consciousness a person brings to the experience probably bears on the resultant effects.

50. How can I avoid unpleasant surroundings and entities while out of body?

You may wish to use some sort of prayer, affirmation, or symbol for protection as you enter into experimentation. Try to bring as much of a feeling of security to your experience as possible.

51. Do I have to be "religious" in order to have this experience?

It appears that this experience can happen any time to any person. This is shown especially in spontaneous cases that have their impetus from accidents, illness, operations, and other crisis situations.

52. What happens if I get back into my body "upside down?"

Whereas there have been reports of people experiencing temporary disorientation, such as being "upside down," they have always been able to make the proper adjustments. Keep trying to reorient yourself to your usual position. Try not to panic and know that you can get yourself in the correct position.

53. Is one always aware of "going" to another place or just suddenly "being" there?

Claims range from moving about in a normal way to traveling through space at inordinate rates of speed to simply being where you desire to be without any knowledge of getting there.

54. Describe the "leaving" sensation of going out of body and the feeling of reentering.

Leaving is sometimes experienced as slipping out of the body with physical sensations, although some reports indicate there is no sense of leaving but only a realization of being at a different point of view. Reentering is similar in that some people experience a jarring sensation of realignment, whereas others merely realize they are back to their original point of view.

55. Will my body be paralyzed while I am away from it?

Many cases include a report of paralysis or catalepsy of the body but some seem to maintain some control in the physical body while perceiving exterior to it. For instance, one report stated that the person perceived himself as walking on one side of the street and looking across and seeing his body walking on the other side.

56. Will I experience physical sensations (such as ringing in ears or bodily vibrations) as clues that I am about to have an OBE?

Sensations such as ringing in the ears or bodily vibrations are sometimes reported. Some report the sensation of falling or rising. It would seem that one's sensitivity to physical sensations may influence one's sensitivity during OBES.

57. Can a person be physically in two places at once (bilocation), doing two different things?

Bilocation is the experience of being two places simultaneously and there have been reports of people having been seen at both places during the same space of time. The case of Alphonso de Liguori is a good example of this. One night in Italy in 1774 this monk was simultaneously seen in his cell and at the bedside of the dying Pope Clement XIV about 100 miles away.

Reports indicate that one is usually quiescent in one place and active in another, but this is not always true. Whereas one may experience being two places at once, reports are less frequent that one is active in both locations. Bilocation is rather like an OBE with independent observers.

58. What is the difference between bilocation and OBE?

The difference in bilocation seems to be the ability to materialize the out-of-body form to such an extent that it can be perceived at both locations doing separate tasks. Bilocation, as defined by Bozzano, "is used to designate the various ways in which the mysterious occurrence of 'exteriorization of the double' takes place in the bodily organism."[7]

59. Is it possible to see the "double" of another person?

Many have reported seeing the double of someone else. One of the most reflected-on reports of this type was the Wilmot case where two individuals perceived the double at the same time from different perspectives. The Doppelgänger phenomenon, reported fairly frequently in Europe, is also an example of seeing the double of another.

60. Can I see the "double" of another person without their knowing they are visible to me?

Whereas some reports indicate that people do realize they are somehow making their out-of-body entity visible to others, it is also not uncommon for someone to report having seen the phantom of a person who had no awareness of being visible at a point distant from his or her body.

61. Can I make myself visible to another person at a distant place?

Hornell Hart cites cases of people who attempted and apparently succeeded in making themselves visible to a distant person.[8] The ability to materialize oneself in an apparitional form some distance away from the body is claimed in many anecdotes, but has not yet been scientifically established.

62. Can I remain undetected when I have an OBE or will people always somehow know that I am there?

It appears that some effort is required to make one's out-of-body presence visible at a distant place and simultaneously be aware that one is doing this. I imagine that one's double usually goes unrecognized by those one visits in an OBE. Whether the phantom is seen or not also seems to depend on the sensitivity of the percipient, including degree of emotional attachment.

63. Can one see through ceilings, walls, or other solid objects during OBEs?

Reports indicate that solid objects can be experienced as intangible during an OBE. Some report that they can not only see through them but move through them quite easily. Others are blocked by solid objects such as walls and doors. We infer from this that there are differences in the out-of-body density.

64. If I have a disability, such as deafness or myopia, will my out-of-body perceptions be impaired also?

People report being able to see clearly while out of body even though their physical eyesight is impaired. Reports of near-death experiences where an OBE takes place indicate that one can be perfectly fit and totally perceptive while the body is unconscious, paralyzed, and lacking vital life signs. Such claims suggest that out-of-body perception is not hampered by physical disabilities.

65. What does the Bible say about the OBE?

Paul wrote in I Corinthians 15:44, "If there is a physical body, there is a spiritual body." The belief that every human being possesses a spiritual body is age old and adds to the foundation of practically all religions. Ecclesiastes wrote of a silver cord, which could be interpreted as the spinal cord, but could refer to the attachment many out-of-body experients report between their physical and astral bodies. They seem to feel this cord sustains physical life and the scripture also states this: "if ever the silver cord be loosed ... the spirit shall return to God who gave it" (Ecc. 12:6-7).

Another story of interest is that of Philip, who had just baptized a eunuch on a desert road between Gaza and Jerusalem, "And when they came up out of the water, the Spirit of the Lord caught up Philip; and the eunuch saw him no more, and went on his way rejoicing. But Philip was found at Azotus" (Acts 8:39-40). This story goes beyond what we normally consider an OBE in that it implies that Philip's body was actually transferred through space approximately 15 miles to another town. Another possibility is that Philip was bilocated and it was his double who baptized the eunuch.

66. Does one need an inner guide to help them with these experiences?

An inner guide does not seem to be essential but people who experiment in depth often report reaching a point where they depend on such guides at times for help, direction, and understanding.

67. What are the main fears that hold one back from an OBE?

The number one fear is that one will not be able to get back "in the body" and will therefore die. This seems to be the major obstacle to a full realization of the experience. Others feel that their becoming aware of themselves as being able to operate independently from the body will not be understood by loved ones and peers. This may create a chasm or lack of understanding between them. A painful spiritual isolation may result, which would be undesirable to most.

68. Could I die from this experience?

If one were to leave the body permanently during an OBE, naturally there would be no report of this. It is a safe assumption that some terminal patients may experience out-of-body states just prior to death. I have heard and read reports of people getting headaches or becoming debilitated or disoriented after considerable practice with OBE. It is possible that one could experience a temporary adverse physical effect even after a first spontaneous experience. Any sudden shock can cause one to feel a bit nauseated.

69. Have astral bodies actually been photographed?

French researchers claimed to have photographed out-of-body entities. Many photographic techniques were devised. It is difficult to interpret the photographs without accurate, detailed descriptions of circumstances at the time they were photographed.

70. Should another person be present while I am trying for an OBE?

If you will feel more comfortable to have another person present during your early experiments then, by all means, make yourself comfortable. It really depends on whether you think the presence of another person will help or hinder your experience.

71. How much effect will my own assumptions and expectations have on my OBE?

If you have certain preconceived expectations about the form your experience should take, this will undoubtedly influence your OBE. It may also prevent you from fully realizing the potential of your experience. If your expectations are extremely limited, this may serve as a denial mechanism to invalidate any aspects of your experience which do not fit into your structured levels of tolerance and acceptance.

72. How can I prevent unwanted, spontaneous OBEs?

Try to occupy your mind with other interests and consciously move away from upsetting or alarming experiences. It may help to talk with a person who understands your dilemma and can help you to realize your own power to control your experience. Having unwanted spontaneous experiences of any kind can only denote a feeling of powerlessness to control and direct one's conscious mental life. Turn your attention to other topics as you reaffirm your own authority over yourself.

73. Will I experience ordinary internal bodily sensations in my nonphysical body?

In cases of OBE during illness, operations, or accidents, experients often report that they feel no physical pain during the experience. Others claim they are aware of physical sensations, including pain, during their OBEs. As with most phenomena experienced during an OBE, individual differences exist across the board. What is true for one experient may be totally opposite to what is true for another person.

74. Will I be able to have joint OBEs with others?

There are reports of people going on astral flights together from the same point of origin or meeting other astral doubles arriving from different places. Yram tells of trips with his wife and Fox tells of setting up meeting with other entities who shared the same purpose of experimentation. In *The Power Within*, Alexander Cannon wrote of an experiment in which he hypnotized two people separately and sent them to the same place to report on what they saw there.

75. Can some people see their physical bodies during an OBE?

Many experients seem to be able to see and identify their physical bodies from their points of view in space. Spontaneous experiences are often of the nature of rising several feet above the body and looking down at the motionless form.

76. Is any physical position especially conducive to having an OBE?

A relaxed position is probably best, as it would appear the less attention or activity of the physical organism, the easier the release. Experients are characteristically detached in their attitudes toward their physical bodies during projection.

77. Can I go from a dream into an OBE?

Many personal experimenters recommend working through dream control to out-of-body states. By paying attention to this common but little understood human experience (dreaming), you can be assured of expanding your awareness of yourself and your abilities. The trick is to bring consciousness to the dream state, exert some control over the dream, and pay close attention to who or what is conscious and controlling at this time.

78. Will I experience emotions during OBEs?

Emotions such as joy, exhilaration, fear, anxiety, love, psychic pain, grief, and curiosity are reported in OBES. People often report a sense of freedom and well-being never before experienced. They also comment on the solidity or reality of the double, identifying it as the real self in the experience, rather than the body.

79. Will I be able to think and make decisions while out of body?

It has been reported by many experients that they not only cognitively process information during an OBE but make decisions and take actions based on those decisions. Correct identification of target material in laboratory experiments requires decision-making abilities.

80. Will I experience aftereffects of an OBE, such as disorientation?

If the OBE is prolonged, it may take longer for you to reorient yourself to physical surroundings. Other aftereffects may include a sense of wonder, self-doubt, a knowledge that life continues after death of the body, or a lack of ability to disclose the event to others because of its ineffability or fear of scorn.

81. If I have had many ESP experiences, will this make it easier for me to have an OBE?

If you are cognizant of your ESP experiences, you should be more able to recognize and validate an OBE.

82. Has a psychological profile been obtained of those who have frequent, controlled OBEs?

Psychological profiles were obtained on remote viewing specialists at Stanford Research Institute; however, this information has not been released. Hundreds of questionnaires have been completed by people who experience OBES and some of the data have been computerized. Again, no analysis or interpretation of these data have been published. Drs. Tart and Osis have accumulated much of it.

83. How do you account for feelings such as elation during an OBE, since in accident cases people who report going out of body often say they feel no pain?

Whereas Celia Green did report an absence of the feeling of physical pain in accident cases, other writers have described painful experiences. It appears emotions and sensations can be felt in OBES. Some of those who go out of body during operations can still feel their bodies in pain, but others experience the body as an objective observer might.

84. Why does out-of-body vision vary in accuracy of perception from time to time?

Clarity of exterior vision does seem to fluctuate from time to time. There are hints that moods, attitudes, physical health, and atmospheric conditions might affect the vision in some ways.

85. Why can some people see a shape but not be able to name what it is during an OBE?

Just as we perceive figure/ground before we read words, it is possible that through individual differences one may be at the stage of figure/ground perception in an OBE, or at that of concept formation.

86. What does it accomplish to have an OBE?

It usually has a profound effect on the rest of the experient's life. There are reports of an added dimension to life
and a loss of the fear of death in numerous cases. Some practical
purposes for which exterior vision might be used are crime detection, natural resource exploration, healing, space exploration, or
finding missing persons or objects.

87. Can having an OBE help me solve my daily problems any better?

Having an OBE may cause you to place less significance on
daily routine problems. Your attitude toward your present
problems is likely to change. As the problems becomes less important in your mind, you will either know you have the ability to
handle them and you will do it or you may decide they are un-
worthy of the time and attention you are giving them. Different
types of problems may replace some mundane problems that are
presently considered of utmost importance.

88. Will any vitamin or nutritional regime facilitate an OBE?

Some personal experimenters state that vitamins and
nutrition play an important role in the quality of the OBE. If you
are interested in this approach, find someone you trust and let
them guide you. Extreme fasting or overdoses of vitamins
without qualified direction could create physical and mental
problems.

89. Is fasting a good way to induce the experience?

Fasting often helps in spiritual growth if it is done correctly. It sometimes leads to experiences of a hallucinatory nature.
The one thing you want to avoid at all costs is self-delusion.

90. Is there 360° vision in an OBE?

Some people report 360° vision in an OBE; some report
being able to see in the opposite direction to which their bodies
are facing. Others describe their vision as if looking through a
fish-eye lens. Most describe a normal angle of vision (often from
above) but with various distortions.

91. Is it important that I be free of emotional conflict before attempting OBEs?

I doubt that anyone can ever be totally free of emotional
conflict but the healthier your mental state as you attempt OBES,
the better off you will be. Imagine being confronted with a

totally new concept of reality and what that might do to an unstable mind. The less anxiety, the more you will be able to pay attention to your experience and learn from it. In spontaneous cases, it is often emotional conflict, trauma, or despair which triggers an OBE. But, in a conscious effort to produce the experience, one should be as relaxed and calm as possible.

End Notes

[1]More questions and comments on OBES can be found in H.B. Greenhouse, *The Book of Psychic Knowledge* (New York: Taplinger, 1973), pp. 160-171.

[2]Celia Green, *Out-of-the-Body Experiences* (New York: Ballantine, 1973).

[3]Raymond Moody, *Life After Life* (New York: Bantam/Mockingbird, 1975).

[4]Oliver Fox, *Astral Projection* (New Hyde Park, N.Y.: University Books, 1962), p. 49.

[5]Gertrude R. Schmeidler, "PK Effects upon Continuously Recorded Temperature," *Journal of the American Society for Psychical Research* 67 (October 1973):325-340.

[6]R.L. Morris, et al., "Studies of Communication during Out-of-Body Experiences," *Journal of the American Society for Psychical Research* 72 (1978):1-21.

[7]Ernesto Bozzano, *Discarnate Influence in Human Life* (London: John M. Watkins, 1938), p. 101.

[8]Hornell Hart, "ESP Projection: Spontaneous Cases and the Experimental Method," *Journal of the American Society for Psychical Research* 48 (1954):121-146. See Table 2.

Bibliography

*(ASPR is American Society for Psychical Research
and SPR is [British] Society for Psychical Research)*

Alvarado, C.S. "The Physical Detection of the Astral Body: An Historical Perspective." *Theta* 8 (1980):4-7.
ASPR Newsletter 12, 14-20, 22, 6 (4). Reports on ASPR research from 1972 to 1980.
Assagioli, Roberto. *The Act of Will*. New York: Penguin Books, 1979.
Bailey, Alice A. *The Externalization of the Hierarchy*. New York: Lucis Pub. Co., 1958.
Barrett, Lady. *Personality Survives Death*. London: Longmans Green, 1937.
Barrett, H.D. *Life Work of Cora L.V. Richmond*. Chicago: Hack & Anderson, 1895.
Bayless, Raymond. *Apparitions and Survival of Death*. New Hyde Park, N.Y.: University Books, 1973.
Black, David. *Ekstacy: Out of the Body Experiences*. Indianapolis: Bobbs-Merrill, 1975. A reporter's perspective on contemporary OBE research and those involved. Easy to read.
Blackmore, Susan. *Parapsychology and Out-of-the-Body Experiences*. London: Society for Psychical Research; East Sussex: Transpersonal Books, 1978. Author is currently working on an OBE book to be published in England by Heinemann in 1982.
Bourguignon, Erika. "Dreams and Altered States of Consciousness in Anthropological Research." In *Psychological Anthropology*, ed. by F.L.K. Hsu (Cambridge, Mass.: Schenkman, 1972).
_____. "The Self, the Behavioral Environment and the Theory of Spirit Possession." In *Context and Meaning in Cultural Anthropology*, ed. by M.E. Spiro (New York: Free Press, 1965).
Bozzano, Ernesto. *Discarnate Influence in Human Life*. London: John M. Watkins, 1938.
Brent, Sandor B. "Deliberately Induced, Premortem, Out-of-Body Experiences: An Experimental and Theoretical Approach." In *Between Life and Death*, ed. by Robert Kastenbaum (New York: Springer, 1979), pp. 89-123.
Broad, C.D. "Dreaming, and Some of Its Implications." *Proceedings SPR* 52 (1959):53-78.

————. *The Mind and Its Place in Nature*. New York: Harcourt, Brace, 1925.

————. "Phantasms of the Living and of the Dead." *Proceedings SPR* **50** (1953):51-66.

Bucke, R.M. *Cosmic Consciousness*. Secaucas, N.J.: Citadel Press, 1973.

Burt, Cyril. *Psychology and Psychical Research*. London: Society for Psychical Research, 1968, pp. 76-90.

Carrington, Hereward. *The Invisible World*. Philadelphia: Ruttle, Shaw & Wetherill, 1946.

————. *Laboratory Investigations into Psychic Phenomena*. Philadelphia: David McKay, n.d.

————. *Modern Psychical Phenomena*. New York: Dodd, Mead, 1919, pp. 146-154.

————. *Your Psychic Powers and How to Develop Them*. New York: Templestar Publishers, 1958, Chapter 10.

Coleman, Stanley M. "The Phantom Double. Its Psychological Significance." *British Journal of Medical Psychology* 14 (1934):254-273. Discusses the idea of the double in the literature of de Maupassant and Dostoevsky.

Cornillier, P.E. *The Survival of the Soul*. London: Kegan Paul, Trench, Trubner, 1921.

Crookall, Robert J. "Astral Traveling." *International Journal of Parapsychology* 8 (1966):472-477. Review of Susy Smith's book, *The Enigma of Out-of-Body Travel*.

————. *Casebook of Astral Projection, 545-746*. New Hyde Park, N.Y.: University Books, 1972.

————. *During Sleep*. London: Theosophical Pub. House, 1964.

————. *The Interpretation of Cosmic and Mystical Experiences*. London: James Clarke, 1969.

————. *Intimations of Immortality*. London: James Clarke, 1965.

————. *The Jung-Jaffé View of Out-of-the-Body Experiences*. London: World Fellowship Press, 1970.

————. *The Mechanisms of Astral Projection*. Moradabad, India: Darshana International, 1968.

————. *More Astral Projections*. Hackensack, N.J.: Wehman, 1964.

————. *The Next World – and the Next*. London: Theosophical Pub. House, 1966.

————. *Out-of-the-Body Experiences*. New Hyde Park, N.Y.: University Books, 1970.

————. "Out-of-the-Body Experiences and Survival." In *Life, Death and Psychical Research*, ed. by J.D. Pearce-Higgins and G.S. Whitby (London: Rider, 1973), pp. 66-88. Cases with commentary.

————. *The Study and Practice of Astral Projection*. New Hyde Park, N.Y.: University Books, 1966.

————. *The Supreme Adventure*. London: James Clarke, 1961.

————. *The Techniques of Astral Projection*. New York: Weiser, n.d.

Cummins, Geraldine. *Mind in Life and Death.* London: Aquarian Press, 1956.

Deecke, L.; Scheid, P.; and Kornhuber, H.H. "Distribution of Readiness Potential, Pre-Motion Positivity and Motor Potential of the Human Cerebral Cortex Preceding Voluntary Finger Movements." *Experimental Brain Research* 7 (1969):158-168.

Dewhurst, Kenneth. "Autoscopic Hallucinations." *Irish Journal of Medical Science* (1954):263-267.

_____, and Pearson, J. "Visual Hallucinations of the Self in Organic Disease." *Journal of Neurology, Neurosurgery and Psychiatry* 18 (1955):53-57. Discusses three cases of autoscopy and their accompanying organic lesions.

Donahoe, James J. *Dream Reality.* Oakland, Calif.: Bench Press, 1974. Brief descriptions of personal experience, Lilly and Monroe experiences and Jung's archetypal interpretation.

Ducasse, C.J. *A Critical Examination of the Belief in a Life After Death.* Springfield, Ill.: Thomas, 1961.

Eastman, Margaret. "Out-of-Body Experiences." *Proceedings SPR* 53 (1962):287-309. Critical analysis of cases. Interesting and well written. Considers causes and physiological characteristics.

Eccles, Sir John C. "The Human Person in Its Two-Way Relationship to the Brain." In *Research in Parapsychology, 1976,* ed. by J.D. Morris, W.G. Roll, and R.L. Morris (Metuchen, N.J.: Scarecrow Press, 1977).

Eisenbud, Jule. *The World of Ted Serios.* New York: William Morrow, 1967, pp. 231-244. Since many of Serios' psychic photos are "shot from above," Eisenbud discusses the possibility that they could be taken during an OBE.

Evans-Wentz, W.Y. *The Tibetan Book of the Dead.* London: Oxford University Press, 1936.

Field, M.J. "Spirit Possession in Ghana." In *African Mediumship and Society,* ed. by J. Beattie and J. Middleton (New York: Africana Publishing, 1970).

Fox, Oliver. *Astral Projection: A Record of Out-of-the-Body Experiences.* New York: University Books, 1962.

_____. "The Pineal Doorway—a Record of Research." *Occult Review* 31(4) April 1920.

Greeley, Andrew M. *The Sociology of the Paranormal: A Reconnaissance.* Beverly Hills, Calif.: Sage Publications, 1975.

Green, Celia. "Ecsomatic Experiences and Related Phenomena." *Journal SPR* 44 (1967):111-130.

_____. *Out of the Body Experiences.* New York: Ballantine, 1973.

Green, E.E.; Ferguson, D.W.; Green, A.M.; and Walters, E.D. "Voluntary Controls Project: Swami Rama. Preliminary Report." Menninger Foundation, June 6, 1970.

Greenhouse, Herbert B. *The Astral Journey.* New York: Doubleday, 1975. Popular book written to give readers a general overview of OBES. Cases and research are discussed in easy-to-read form.

_____. *The Book of Psychic Knowledge.* New York: Taplinger, 1973, pp. 160-171.

Grosso, Michael. "Plato and Out-of-the-Body Experiences." *Journal ASPR* **69** (1975):61-74. Philosophical article which considers Plato's *Phaedo* and OBES.

_____. "Some Varieties of Out-of-Body Experience." *Journal ASPR* **70** (1976):179-183.

Hall, Preston. "Digest of Spirit Teachings Received Through Mrs. Minnie E. Keeler." *Journal ASPR* **10** (1916):632-660, 679-708.

_____. "Experiments in Astral Projection." *Journal ASPR* **22** (1918): 39-60.

Hart, Hornell. "ESP Projection: Spontaneous Cases and the Experimental Method." *Journal ASPR* **48** (1954):121-146.

_____. "Hypnosis As an Aid in Experimental ESP Projection." Paper read at First International Conference of Parapsychological Studies, Utrecht, 1953.

_____. "Six Theories about Apparitions." *Proceedings SPR* **50** (1956):153-239.

_____. "Travelling ESP." In *Proceedings of the First International Conference of Parapsychological Studies* (New York: Parapsychology Foundation, 1955).

Hartwell, J.; Janis, J.; and Harary, B. "A Study of the Physiological Variables Associated with Out-of-Body Experiences." In *Research in Parapsychology 1974*, ed. by W.G. Roll and R.L. Morris (Metuchen, N.J.: Scarecrow Press, 1975), pp. 127-129. No unique physiological indicators of the OBE state emerged in this study.

Heywood, Rosalind. "Correspondence: Out-of-the-Body Experiences." *Journal SPR* (June 1963):86. Incidence of OBE discussed.

Irwin, H.J. "Out of the Body Down Under: Some Cognitive Characteristics of Australian Students Reporting OBES." *Journal SPR* **50** (1980):448-459.

James, William. *The Will to Believe.* New York: Dover, 1956.

Jordan, David Starr. "The Posthom Phantom: A Study in the Spontaneous Activity of Shadows." *Science* 9 (May 12, 1899):674-681.

Landau, Lucian. "An Unusual Out-of-the-Body Experience." *Journal SPR* **42** (1963):126-128.

Larsen, Caroline D. *My Travels in the Spirit World.* Rutland, Vt.: Tuttle, 1927.

Lee, S.G. "Spirit Possession Among the Zulu." In *African Mediumship and Society*, ed. by J. Beattie and J. Middleton (New York: Africana Publishing, 1970).

Lehmann, Heinz E. "Unusual Psychiatric Disorders and Atypical Psychoses." In *Comprehensive Textbook of Psychiatry — II*, ed. by A. Freedman, H. Kaplan, and B. Sadock (Baltimore: Williams & Wilkins, 1975).

Leonard, Gladys Osborne. *My Life in Two Worlds.* London: Cassell, 1931. Subjective reporting of this famous medium's extraterrestrial experiences.

Lhermitte, Jean. "Visual Hallucination of the Self." *British Medical Journal* 1 (1951):431-434. Points out that this is the only hallucination where people feel they are a part of the image or double, thereby distinguishing this experience from any other sensory hallucination. It is a treat to browse through this journal.

Lilly, John C. *The Center of the Cyclone.* New York: Bantam Books, 1972. Fairly interesting account of some of his work with dolphins, but more on his experiences under LSD. He reports on "spaces" he was able to get into using meditation and other techniques at Esalen and Arica, Chile. If you have not had the experiences, his subjective reporting is not convincing.

Lippman, Caro W. "Hallucinations of Physical Duality in Migraine." *Journal of Nervous and Mental Disease* 117 (1953):345-350.

Lukianowicz, N. "Autoscopic Phenomena." *AMA Archives of Neurological Psychiatry* 80 (1958):199-220. Most descriptive article on the autoscopic experience, including cases. Discussion of causes and psychological theory.

McDougall, D. "Hypothesis Concerning Soul Substance Together with Experimental Evidence of the Existence of Such Substance." *Journal ASPR* 1 (1907):237-244.

McIntosh, A.I. "Beliefs About Out-of-the-Body Experiences Among the Elema, Gulf Kamea and Rigo Peoples of Papua New Guinea." *Journal SPR* 50 (1980):460-477.

Mead, G.R.S. *The Doctrine of the Subtle Body in Western Tradition.* London: Stuart & Watkins, 1919.

Mischel, W., and Mischel, F. "Psychological Aspects of Spirit Possession." *American Anthropologist* 60 (1958):249-260.

Mishlove, Jeffrey. *The Roots of Consciousness.* New York: Random House, 1975, pp. 126-138. Fast-paced, easy-to-read, and beautifully illustrated overview of various types of phenomena. Not always totally accurate on OBES.

Mitchell, Janet Lee. "Out-of-Body Experiences and Autoscopy." *The Osteopathic Physician*, April 1974, pp. 44-49. Compares the two phenomena.

————. "Out-of-the-Body Vision." *Psychic*, April 1973, pp. 44-47. Report on ASPR experiments with Swann.

————. "A Psychic Probe of the Planet Mercury." *Psychic*, June 1975, pp. 16-21. Compares Swann and Sherman psychic data with feedback from spacecraft Mariner 10 probing Mercury.

Monroe, Robert A. *Journeys Out of the Body.* New York: Doubleday, 1971.

Moody, Raymond. *Life After Life.* New York: Bantam/Mockingbird, 1975.

Morris, R.L. "PRF Research on Out-of-Body Experiences, 1973." *Theta* 41 (1974):1-3. Popular version of the entry below.

————. "The Use of Detectors for Out-of-Body Experiences." In *Research in Parapsychology 1973*, ed. by W.G. Roll, R.L. Morris, and J.D. Morris (Metuchen, N.J.: Scarecrow Press, 1974), pp.

114-116. The use of human, animal, and physiological detectors in experiments with Blue Harary.

————; Harary, S.B.; Janis, J.; Hartwell, J.; and Roll, W.G. "Studies of Communication During Out-of-Body Experiences." *Journal ASPR* **72** (1978):1-21.

Moss, Thelma. *The Probability of the Impossible.* Los Angeles: J.P. Tarcher, 1974, pp. 278-304. Kirlian photography and acupuncture are topics of main interest to this parapsychologist. Her section on OBES is sparse and just hits high points as a general introduction to the subject.

Muldoon, Sylvan. *The Case for Astral Projection.* Chicago: Aries Press, 1936.

————. *The Projection of the Astral Body.* New York: Weiser, n.d. Muldoon was one of the first in this country to write about his experiences. His books are classics in that they contain early cases, techniques, and theorizing. Interesting and easy to read.

————, and Carrington, H. *The Phenomena of Astral Projection.* New York: Weiser, n.d.

Myers, F.W.H. "Note on a Suggested Mode of Psychical Interaction." In *Phantasms of the Living,* vol. 2, ed. by Edmund Gurney, F.W.H. Myers, and Frank Podmore (London: Society for Psychical Research, 1886).

Nemiah, John C. "Depersonalization Neurosis." In *Comprehensive Textbook of Psychiatry — II,* ed. by A. Freedman, H. Kaplan, and B. Sadock (Baltimore: Williams & Wilkins, 1975).

Noyes, Russell, Jr. "The Experience of Dying." *Psychiatry* **35** (1972): 174-184.

————. "The Experience of Dying from Falls." *Omega* **3** (1972):45-52.

————, and Slymen, D.J. "The Subjective Response to Life-Threatening Danger." *Omega* **9**(4) (1978-1979):313-321.

Ophiel (pseudonym for LaPeach, E.). *The Art and Practice of Astral Projection.* San Francisco: Peach Pub. Co., 1961.

Osis, Karlis. "Perceptual Experiments on Out-of-Body Experiences." In *Research in Parapsychology 1974,* ed. by J.D. Morris, W.G. Roll, and R.L. Morris (Metuchen, N.J.: Scarecrow Press, 1975), pp. 53-55.

————. "Perspectives for Out-of-Body Research." In *Research in Parapsychology 1973,* ed. by W.G. Roll, R.L. Morris, and J.D. Morris (Metuchen, N.J.: Scarecrow Press, 1974), pp. 110-113.

————. "Toward a Methodology for Experiments on Out-of-the Body Experiences." In *Research in Parapsychology 1972,* ed. by W.G. Roll, R.L. Morris, and J.D. Morris (Metuchen, N.J.: Scarecrow Press, 1973), pp. 78-79. Suggests alternatives for testing the properties of spatial organization of OBE perception.

————, and Haraldsson, E. *At the Hour of Death.* New York: Avon Books, 1977.

————, and McCormick, Donna. "Insiders' Views of the OBE." *ASPR*

Newsletter 4 (3) (July 1978):9.

_____, and _____. "Kinetic Effects at the Ostensible Location of an Out-of-Body Projection During Perceptual Testing." *Journal ASPR* 74 (1980):319-329.

_____, and Mitchell, J.L. "Physiological Correlates of Reported Out-of-Body Experiences." *Journal SPR* 49 (1977):525-536.

_____, and Perskari, Boneita. "Perceptual Tests of the Out-of-Body Hypothesis." Report distributed by the Chester F. Carlson Research Laboratory, ASPR, 1975.

Ostow, Mortimer. "The Metapsychology of Autoscopic Phenomena." *Journal of Psychoanalysis* 41 (1960): 619-625.

"'Out-of-the-Body' Experience." *Journal ASPR* 34 (1938):206-211. Case reported through correspondence.

Owen, Robert Dale. *Footfalls on the Boundary of Another World.* London: Trubner, 1860.

Oxenham, John. *Out of the Body.* London: Longmans, Green, 1941.

Palmer, John. "Consciousness Localized in Space Outside the Body." *The Osteopathic Physician*, April 1974, pp. 51-62. Introductory-type article written for medical personnel, but interesting and easy-to-read data for general readers, as well.

_____. "The Out-of-Body Experience: A Psychological Theory." *Parapsychology Review* 9(5) (1978):19-22.

_____, and Lieberman, R. "The Influence of Psychological Set on ESP and Out-of-Body Experiences." *Journal ASPR* 69 (1975):193-213.

_____, and Vassar, C. "ESP and Out-of-the-Body Experiences: An Exploratory Study," *Journal ASPR* 68 (1974):257-280.

Panati, Charles. *Supersenses.* New York: Quadrangle/New York Times Book Co., 1974, pp. 139-150. Summaries of OBE experiments. Fairly reliable data; easy to read.

Powell, Arthur E. *The Astral Body and Other Astral Phenomena.* Wheaton, Ill.: Theosophical Pub. House, 1973. This is one in a series of Quest Books by this author. Other books in the series include *The Etheric Double and Allied Phenomena, The Mental Body*, and *The Causal Body and the Ego.*

Prevost-Battersby, H.F. *Man Outside Himself: The Methods of Astral Projection.* New Hyde Park, N.Y.: University Books, 1969. Good case reporting and careful consideration of data. Easily readable, concise, and informative.

Reyes, B.F. *Scientific Evidence of the Existence of the Soul.* Wheaton, Ill.: Theosophical Pub. House, 1970, pp. 179-191. Case analysis and personal experience. Concludes that consciousness can function outside the body and is completely independent of the brain.

Richmond, Cora L.V. *My Experiences While Out of My Body.* Boston: Christopher Pub. House, 1923.

Ring, Kenneth. *Life at Death: A Scientific Investigation of the Near-Death Experience.* New York: Coward, McCann, and Geoghegan, 1980.

Rogo, D. Scott. "Aspects of Out-of-the-Body Experiences." *Journal SPR* **48** (1976):329-335.

————. "Astral Projection in Tibetan Buddhist Literature." *International Journal of Parapsychology* **10** (1968):277-284. Discusses OBES cited in ancient Tibetan writings.

————. *An Experience of Phantoms.* New York: Taplinger, 1974. Contains quite a bit of data on OBES, including some of the methods used to induce the experience and some of the possible dangers.

————. "A Haunting by a Living Agent." *Theta* **6**(2 & 3) (1978): 15-20.

————. *Mind Beyond the Body.* New York: Penguin, 1978.

————. "Out-of-the-Body Experiences." *Psychic*, April 1973, pp. 50-55. Gives brief summary of cases and research done. Informative and well written.

————. *Parapsychology: A Century of Inquiry.* New York: Taplinger, 1975, pp. 273-277. Considers the OBE as possible evidence for survival.

————. *The Welcoming Silence.* Secaucus, N.J.: University Books, 1973, pp. 13-50. Usual good summary of primary data and description of his personal OBES.

Roll, W.G.; Morris, R.L.; Harary, Blue; Wells, Roger; and Hartwell, John. "Further OBE Experiments with a Cat As Detector." In *Research in Parapsychology 1974*, ed. by J.D. Morris, W.G. Roll, and R.L. Morris (Metuchen, N.J. Scarecrow Press, 1975), pp. 55-56.

Sabom, Michael B. *Recollections of Death: A Medical Investigation.* New York: Harper & Row (in press).

Schmeidler, Gertrude R. "PK Effects upon Continuously Recorded Temperature." *Journal ASPR* **67** (October 1973):325-340.

Sewall, May (Wright). *Neither Dead nor Sleeping.* Indianapolis: Bobbs-Merrill, 1920.

Sherman, Harold. *How to Make ESP Work for You.* Greenwich, Conn.: Fawcett, 1964, pp. 129-155.

————. *Your Mysterious Powers of ESP.* New York: New American Library, 1969.

Sherman, Spencer. "Brief Report: Very Deep Hypnosis." *Journal of Transpersonal Psychology* **1** (1972):87-91.

Shiels, Dean. "A Cross-Cultural Study of Beliefs in Out-of-the-Body Experiences." *Journal SPR* **49** (1978):697-741.

Shirley, Ralph. *The Mystery of the Human Double.* New Hyde Park, N.Y.: University Books, 1965.

Sidgwick, Eleanor M. "On the Evidence for Clairvoyance." *Proceedings SPR* **7** (1891-1892):41-47.

Siegel, R.K. "The Psychology of Life After Death." *American Psychologist* **35**:10 (October 1980):911-931.

Smith, Susy. *The Enigma of Out-of-Body Travel.* New York: New American Library, 1965. A valuable introduction to the subject. It contains important case histories and unbiased scientific, as well as personal thoughts, on the varying phenomena. Easy to read, enjoyable, and informative. Good index and bibliography.

_____. *Out-of-Body Experiences for the Millions*. Los Angeles: Shelbourne Press, 1968.

Stratton, F.J.M. "An Out-of-the-Body Experience Combined with ESP." *Journal SPR* 39 (1957):92-97. Report of a spontaneous case.

Swann, Ingo. *To Kiss Earth Good-Bye*. New York: Hawthorn Books, Inc., 1975.

Tanous, Alex, with Ardman, Harvey. *Beyond Coincidence*. New York: Doubleday, 1976.

Targ, R., and Puthoff, H. "Information Transmission under Conditions of Sensory Shielding." *Nature* 251 (1974): 602-607.

_____, and _____. *Mind-Reach*. New York: Delacorte Press, 1977. The above article and this book describe experiments in remote viewing conducted by these two physicists at Stanford Research Institute.

Tart, Charles. *On Being Stoned*. Palo Alto, Calif.: Science and Behavior Books, 1971.

_____. "Out-of-the-Body Experiences." In *Psychic Exploration*, ed. by E.D. Mitchell (New York: Putnam, 1974), pp. 349-373.

_____. "A Psychophysiological Study of Out-of-the-Body Experiences in a Selected Subject." *Journal ASPR* 62 (1968):3-27.

_____. "Reviews." *Journal ASPR* 64 (1970):271-277. Book reviews of Celia Green's *Lucid Dreams* and *Out-of-the-Body Experiences*.

_____. "A Second Psychophysiological Study of Out-of-the-Body Experiences in a Gifted Subject." *International Journal of Parapsychology* 9 (1967):251-258.

Thomas, C. Drayton. *Life Beyond Death with Evidence*. London: W. Collins, 1928.

Todd, J., and Dewhurst, K. "The Double: Its Psychopathology and Psycho-Physiology." *Journal of Nervous and Mental Disease* 122 (1955):47-55.

Turvey, Vincent. *The Beginnings of Seership: Astral Projection, Clairvoyance and Prophecy*. New Hyde Park, N.Y.: University Books, 1969.

Tylor, E.B. *Primitive Culture*. London: J. Murray, 1871.

Tyrrell, G.N.M. *Apparitions*. New York: Macmillan, 1963, pp. 165-171. Report of five cases of OBE during near-death circumstances.

Van Eeden, Frederik. "A Study of Dreams." *Proceedings SPR* 26 (1913):431-461. Also in *Altered States of Consciousness*, ed. by Charles Tart (Garden City, N.Y.: Doubleday, 1972), pp. 147-160.

Walkenstein, Eileen. "The Death Experience in Insulin Coma Treatment." *American Journal of Psychiatry* 112 (1956).

Walker, Benjamin. *Beyond the Body — The Human Double and the Astral Planes*. London: Routledge & Kegan Paul, 1974.

Wereide, Thorstein. "Norway's Human Doubles." *Tomorrow* 3 (2) (1955):23-29.

Whiteman, J.H. M. "Evidence of Survival from 'Other World' Experiences." *Journal ASPR* 59 (1965):160-166.

————. *The Mystical Life*. London: Faber & Faber, 1961.

————. "The Process of Separation and Return in Experiences Fully 'Out-of-the-Body'." *Proceedings SPR* 50 (1956):240-274.

Whitton, J.L. "'Ramp Functions' in EEG Power Spectra During Actual or Attempted Paranormal Events." *New Horizons* 1 (1974):174-183.

Yram. *Practical Astral Projection*. New York: Weiser, 1974.

Zubek, J.P., ed. *Sensory Deprivation: Fifteen Years of Research*. New York: Appleton-Century-Crofts, 1969.

Index

125